United States
Department of
Agriculture

Forest Service

**Southern Research
Station**

General Technical
Report SRS—164

Predicted High-Water Elevations for Selected Flood Events at the Albert Pike Recreation Area, Ouachita National Forest

Daniel A. Marion

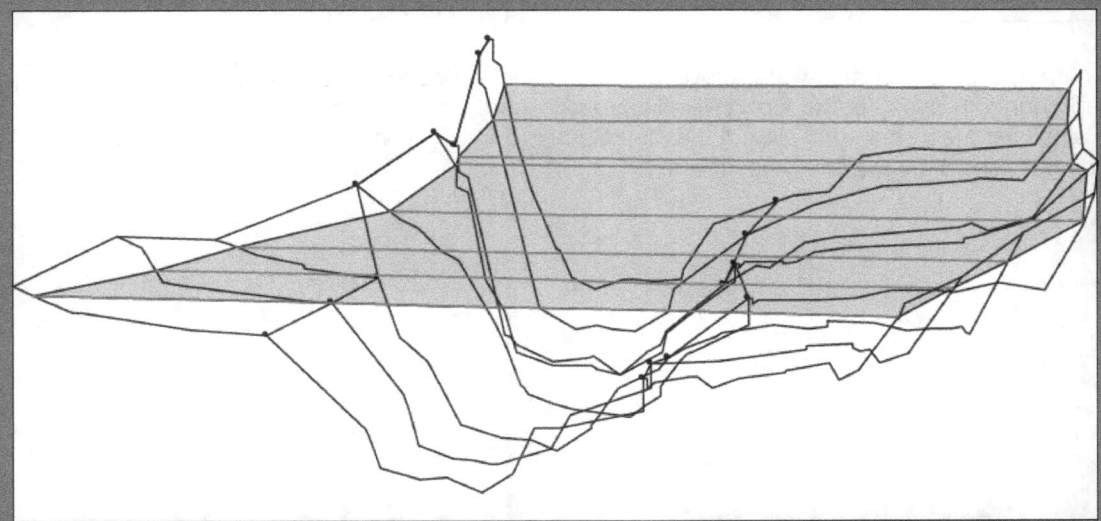

The Author:

Daniel A. Marion, Research Hydrologist, U.S. Department of Agriculture Forest Service, Southern Research Station, Center for Bottomland Hardwoods Research Work Unit, Hot Springs, AR 71902.

Cover Graph:

Three-dimensional plot of high-water elevations (light blue) produced by the June 11, 2010, flood in Campgrounds B and C of the Albert Pike Recreation Area near Langley, AR. Campground B is on the small flat area on the left side of the plot; Campground C is on the much larger flat area on the right side. The view is looking upstream.

September 2012

Predicted High-Water Elevations for Selected Flood Events at the Albert Pike Recreation Area, Ouachita National Forest

Daniel A. Marion

Contents

Predicted High-Water Elevations for Selected Flood Events at the Albert Pike Recreation Area, Ouachita National Forest

Daniel A. Marion

Note to reader: While this publication describes a study that predicts the high-water elevations for selected flood events at the Albert Pike Recreation Area in Arkansas, it may be helpful to know what is *not* addressed. This study does not address how storm patterns, precipitation characteristics, drainage pattern, or past changes in upstream vegetation cover and road density might affect the occurrence, magnitude, timing, or frequency of flooding at the Recreation Area.

ABSTRACT

The hydraulic characteristics are determined for the June 11, 2010, flood on the Little Missouri River at the Albert Pike Recreation Area in Arkansas. These characteristics are then used to predict the high-water elevations for the 10-, 25-, 50-, and 100-year flood events in the Loop B, C, and D Campgrounds of the recreation area. The peak discharge and related roughness characteristics of the June 11, 2010, flood are determined using detailed field survey data and iterative slope-area modeling, while standard step modeling is used to assess the fit of computed to observed high-water elevations. Results show that the peak discharge during the flood was 35,600 cubic feet per second in the upper portion of the Loop D Campground, and 40,800 cubic feet per second in the lower portion of the Loop D and all of the Loop B and C Campgrounds. Peak discharges for the 10-, 25-, 50-, and 100-year flood events are computed using regional-regression equations. Standard step modeling of high-water elevations for the 10-, 25-, 50-, and 100-year discharges shows that the Loop C and D Campgrounds are located at or below the 10-year flood elevation, and that the Loop B Campground is located close to the 25-year flood elevation. The elevations of the Loop B, C, and D Campgrounds averaged 1 to 7 feet below the computed 100-year flood high-water elevations.

Keywords: 100-year flood, Albert Pike Recreation Area campground, Manning *n* estimation, peak discharge, regional-regression equation, slope-area method, standard step method.

INTRODUCTION

This study was undertaken to accurately determine the elevations of selected flood events within the Albert Pike Recreation Area (APRA) near Langley, AR. The APRA consists of four separate campground areas designated as Loops A, B, C, and D (fig. 1). On June 11, 2010, a flash flood occurred on the Little Missouri River (LMR) that damaged or destroyed much of the campground developments in the APRA and killed 20 campers. Using observations of the high-water marks produced by this flash flood (hereafter referred to as the "11 June event" or "11 June flood"), along with detailed measurements of the terrain and ground cover, the hydraulic variables that determine the high-water elevation (HWE) can be quantified and used to predict the HWE for any other flood discharge.

The objective of this study is to determine the HWEs of the peak discharge for the 10-, 25-, 50-, and 100-year flood events within the APRA and assess how these elevations compare to ground elevations of the existing Loop B, C, and D Campgrounds. First, the hydraulic roughness characteristics and peak discharge for the 11 June flood are computed based on the observed high-water marks for this event. Then these roughness characteristics are used to model the HWEs that would occur in the Loop B, C, and D Campgrounds during the 10-, 25-, 50-, and 100-year flood events.

This report documents the methods used in this study, how these methods were applied, and the results obtained. A discussion of factors affecting how much confidence can be placed in these results is also included. The intended audience for this report includes hydrologists and related resource scientists, engineers, forest planners, and forest managers. A glossary is provided to define terms that may be unfamiliar to some readers.

STUDY AREA

Ouachita Mountains

The Albert Pike Recreation Area (APRA) is located in the southern portion of the Ouachita Mountains. The Ouachita Mountains are a series of east-west trending, parallel ridges composed of alternating, intermixed beds of sandstone and shale that are highly folded and faulted. These formations are of Paleozoic age and were first exposed over 300 million years ago. Major streams in the region generally follow joints that occur within the underlying rock strata. The climate throughout the Ouachita Mountains is humid subtropical with warm winters, hot summers, and relatively high annual rainfall (mean = 54 inches) that is evenly distributed throughout the year. The region is located where relatively dry, cold continental air frequently interacts with warm, moist Gulf of Mexico air masses. The interaction of these air masses can produce intense thunderstorms, ice storms, tropical storms, and tornados. One such intense storm produced the rainfall that caused the 11 June flood at the APRA.

Basin and Site Description

The APRA is located on the Little Missouri River (LMR) approximately 5 miles north of Langley, AR, where State Highway 369 ends and Forest Service Road (FS Rd) 73 begins (fig. 1). At the bridge where FS Rd 106 crosses the LMR, the LMR drainage basin area is 34.0 square miles. (Hereafter, the LMR watershed upstream of the FS Rd 106 bridge is called the "upper LMR basin"). While the LMR drains the largest portion of the basin, there are two major tributary streams, Long Creek and Brier Creek, which join the LMR upstream of the FS Rd 106 bridge (fig. 1) and drain 11.0 and 3.6 square miles of the upper LMR basin, respectively.

The geologic composition of the upper LMR basin is dominated by the Stanley Formation and Arkansas Novaculite lithologic units (see Geologic map of the Big Fork Quadrangle, Montgomery and Polk counties, Arkansas 2010). The Stanley Formation is composed mostly of shale rock types with some intermixed sandstones, and underlies the valley bottoms and lower slopes of all of the main tributaries. The Arkansas Novaculite unit consists of various colored novaculites which form the upper slopes and

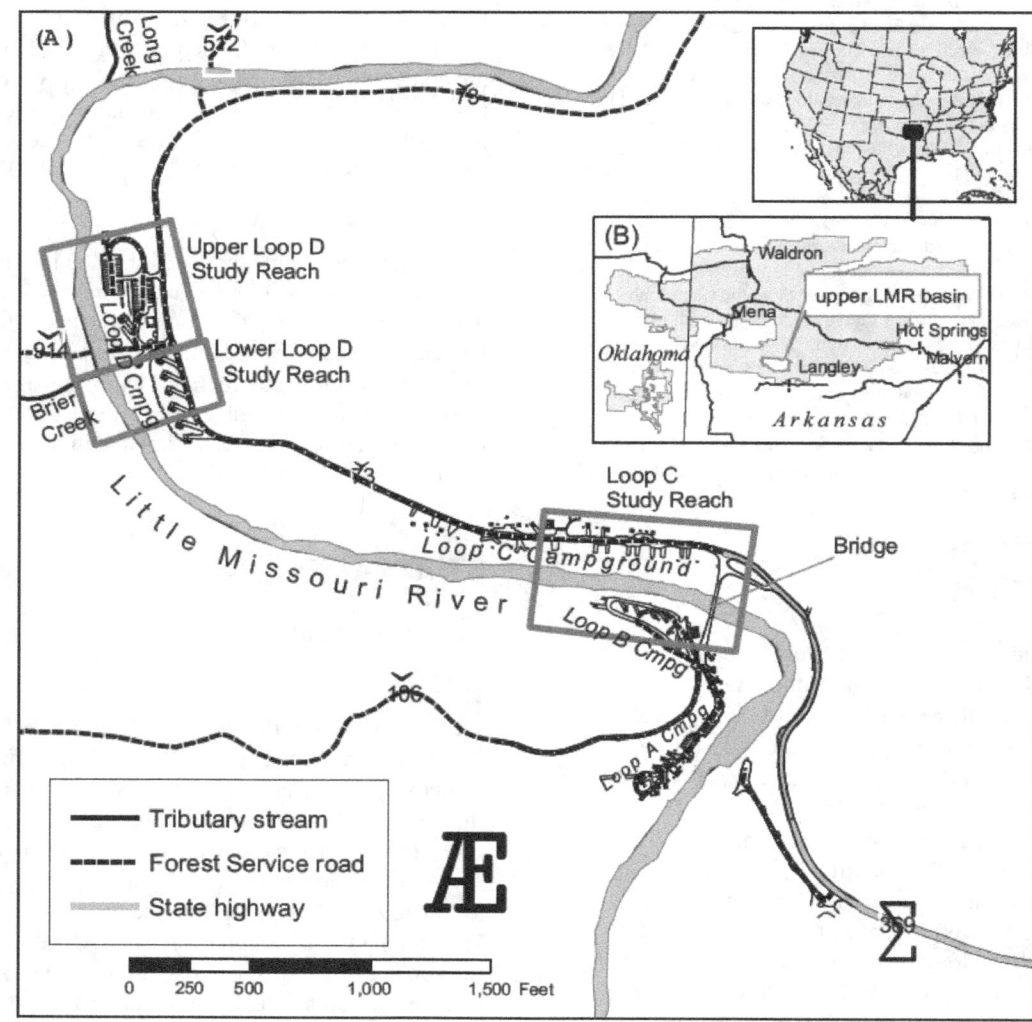

Figure 1   (A) Location of the campgrounds and study reaches in the Albert Pike Recreation Area
(B) Location of the upper Little Missouri River (LMR) basin in the Ouachita National Forest

major ridgelines throughout the basin. Lesser amounts of the Bigfork Formation, Blaylock Formation, and Missouri Mountain Shale-Polk Creek Shale units occur, primarily along secondary ridgelines and main-valley sideslopes. These units consist mostly of various intermixed shales or sandstones of varying bed thicknesses and colors.

Geologic structure greatly influences stream locations and the overall drainage pattern in the upper LMR basin. The ridgelines separating the major tributaries all trend east-west with elevations ranging from 1,600 to 2,200 feet above mean sea level. Thrust faults often occur along or near the contacts between the major lithologic units, and parallel the major ridgelines. The main tributary valleys and streams in the upper LMR basin all follow or parallel these major structural features, giving the composite basin a trellis drainage pattern which is typical of most Ouachita Mountain watersheds. Relief in the major subbasins varies from 500 to 800 feet, and hillslope gradients generally vary from 1 to 3 percent on floodplains and terraces, to 35 percent on the lower slopes, and up to 70 percent on main-valley slopes.

Soils in the upper LMR basin are predominantly medium-textured, well-drained, stony Hapludults, Paleudalfs, or Dystrudepts (Olson 2003, Olson 2007). These soils have a udic moisture regime, fine to loamy-skeletal structure, a thermic temperature regime, and siliceous or mixed mineralogy. Soil depths generally vary inversely with slope and elevation, with shallow to moderate soils depths on steeper slopes and higher ridges, and moderately deep to deep soils occurring on lower slopes and valley bottoms. The vegetation is comprised of pine-hardwood, pine, and oak-hickory forest types whose overstory trees are generally 50 years old or older. Forest cover is generally continuous throughout the upper LMR basin.

The APRA sits along the banks of the LMR between the confluence of Long Creek with the LMR and the junction of State Highway 369 with FS Rd 73 (fig. 1). The Loop A Campground is on the right bank of the LMR just downstream of the FS Rd 106 bridge. (When used to describe channel or reach locations, the terms "left" and "right" are based on facing downstream in the direction of streamflow.) Loops B and C Campgrounds are along the same section of the LMR immediately upstream of the FS Rd 106 bridge. The Loop B Campground is on the right bank, and Loop C Campground on the left bank. The Loop D Campground is approximately 1,500 feet upstream of Loop C, and is also on the left bank.

Within the APRA, the LMR flows in a channel that exhibits both alluvial features and structural control, a

combination that is common in Ouachita Mountain streams. A substantial portion of the active channel bed is covered by discontinuous bedrock exposures, while the remainder is covered by a gravel- to cobble-size substrate. Bedrock exposures are infrequent in the channel banks. Lateral bars and flood-plain patches occur sporadically but are small in extent and poorly developed, suggesting little lateral migration of the channel during the last several 100 years or more. Bank slopes above the active channel often rise well above the bankfull elevation before a distinct slope break occurs.

METHODS

Study Reaches

This analysis models flood elevations in the Loops B, C, and D Campgrounds of the Albert Pike Recreation Area (APRA). Resources for this study were not sufficient to analyze the entire APRA. Small portions of the Loops B, C, and D Campgrounds (described below) were excluded to reduce the required field work while still allowing coverage of the majority of each area. These excluded portions are all close enough to the analyzed areas that high-water elevations (HWEs) can be extrapolated to them with confidence. Resource constraints also lead to all of the Loop A Campground being excluded. It was reasoned that the knowledge gained in modeling the Loops B, C, and D Campgrounds would greatly facilitate later modeling of the Loop A Campground HWEs, if this was desired.

Because of their adjacency, the Loop B and C Campground areas are analyzed together. The analysis reach begins about 180 feet upstream of where the FS Rd 106 bridge crosses the Little Missouri River (LMR), and extends upstream approximately 1,000 feet. This reach is referred to as the Loop C study reach. Within this reach, the valley bottom width expands where the Loop B Campground occurs (fig. 2), but this expansion was not large enough to significantly affect the analysis. The reach contains approximately 75 percent of the Loop C Campground (the three westernmost campsites are excluded) and 75 percent of Loop B (the two easternmost campsites are excluded).

The Loop D Campground area is divided into two reaches for analysis because roughly half of the Loop D Campground area lies upstream of the confluence of Brier Creek with the LMR, while the other half lies downstream (fig. 1). As flow contributed by Brier Creek significantly increases the LMR streamflow volume below this confluence, two reaches are used for the analysis. The valley

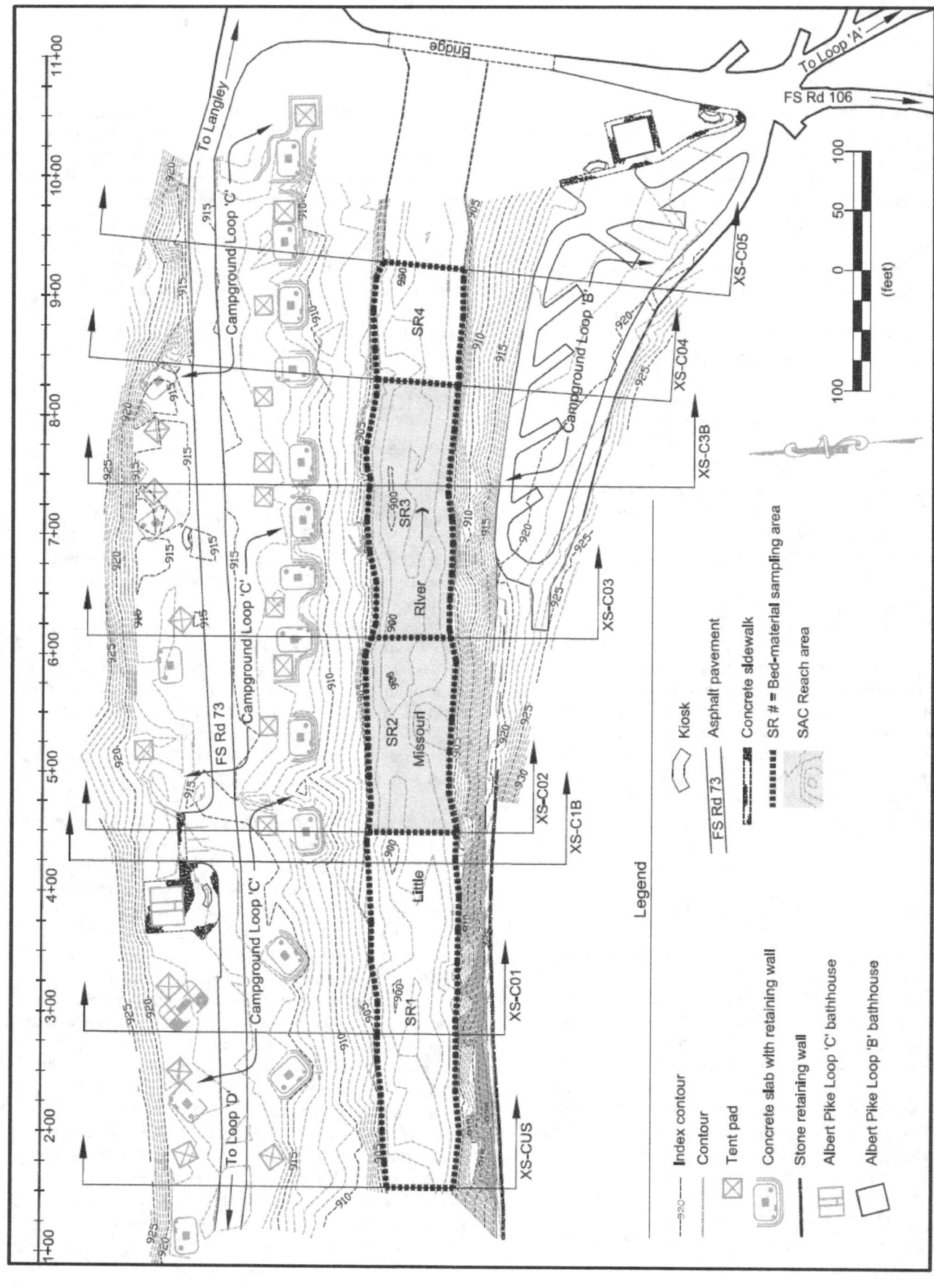

Figure 2 — The Loop C study reach and associated baseline, cross sections, bed-material sampling areas, and campground developments in the Albert Pike Recreation Area. For clarity, the extent of the slope-area computation reach is only shown within the active channel.

bottom width also constricts somewhat where Brier Creek joins the LMR.

The upstream reach, referred to as the Upper Loop D study reach, extends from the Brier Creek confluence to about 700 feet upstream on the LMR. The downstream reach starts at the Brier Creek confluence and extends about 300 feet downstream on the LMR, and is designated the Lower Loop D study reach. The combined Upper and Lower Loop D study reaches encompass about 90 percent of the Loop D Campground (the two southernmost campsites are excluded).

General Analysis Procedure

A key assumption of this analysis is that the roughness values determined for the 11 June flood are the same roughness values that would occur in any flood where the streamflow is sufficient to escape the main channel and inundate the adjacent overbank areas. This is a standard assumption in an analysis such as this one. Benson and Dalrymple (1967) state that roughness becomes constant when flow depths are greater than five times the size of roughness elements and flow width is large relative to flow depth. As will be shown in the Results and Discussion section, any streamflow that overtops the main channel in the three study reaches will meet or exceed both of these requirements.

The analysis procedure follows the steps listed below. These steps were applied separately to the Loop C and Upper Loop D study reaches.

1. Channel geometry, roughness values, and HWEs for the 11 June event are determined using cross sections and other data derived from topographic mapping of the study areas.

2. A preliminary peak discharge "model" is computed for the 11 June flood by applying the slope-area method (Dalrymple and Benson 1967) to a portion of the study reach. Hereafter, when referring to specific peak discharge estimates computed using the slope-area method, the term "model" is used broadly to include both the input data used (the locations, geometry, roughness values, and HWEs of the cross-sections) and the computed outputs (peak discharge and associated hydraulic metrics).

3. Additional candidate models are identified by systematically varying roughness values, recomputing the peak discharge for the same section of the reach, and selecting the three or four models that produce the most confident model predictions.

4. Using the discharge and roughness values for each model from Step 3 (above), the HWEs at all cross sections within the entire reach are computed using a standard step analysis (Brunner 2010b). This is done to assess how well the computed HWEs for each model fit the observed HWEs at all cross sections in the reach. The model that produces the best fit is selected as providing the best estimate of the peak discharge for the 11 June event and the roughness values associated with each cross section.

5. The peak discharges for the 10-, 25-, 50-, and 100-year flood events are computed using the appropriate flood-frequency models for the LMR from the U.S. Geological Survey (1998).

6. Using the peak discharge for each flood from Step 5 and the roughness values from the model selected in Step 4, the HWEs are computed for each of the flood discharges at all cross sections in the study reach using the standard step method.

A different procedure was used for the Lower Loop D study reach. A separate peak discharge model for the 11 June event was not determined for this reach because its discharge is assumed to be the same as that for the Loop C study reach. The Lower Loop D study reach was not used in selecting the best discharge model for the Loop C study reach (Step 4), but the fit of the selected model for Loop C was tested in the Lower Loop D study reach. The same peak discharges for the 10-, 25-, 50-, and 100-year flood events in the Loop C study reach also were used in the Lower Loop D study reach. The change in HWE between the Upper and Lower Loop D study reaches was determined using linear interpolation between the downstream-most cross section in the Upper Loop D study reach and the upstream-most cross section in the Lower Loop D study reach.

Additional details on these procedures and field data collection are given in the following pages.

Field Data Collection

Detailed field surveys were done in the areas of the study reaches to develop high-resolution maps of topography, ground-surface cover types, and high-water marks produced by the 11 June event (figs. 2 and 3). This field work was done between mid-July and mid-August of 2010, approximately 1 month after the 11 June event. Both areas were surveyed using a 20- by 20-foot grid (measured by pacing) with additional survey points wherever topography, ground cover, or channel features changed significantly. Also, numerous campground features (e.g., parking lots,

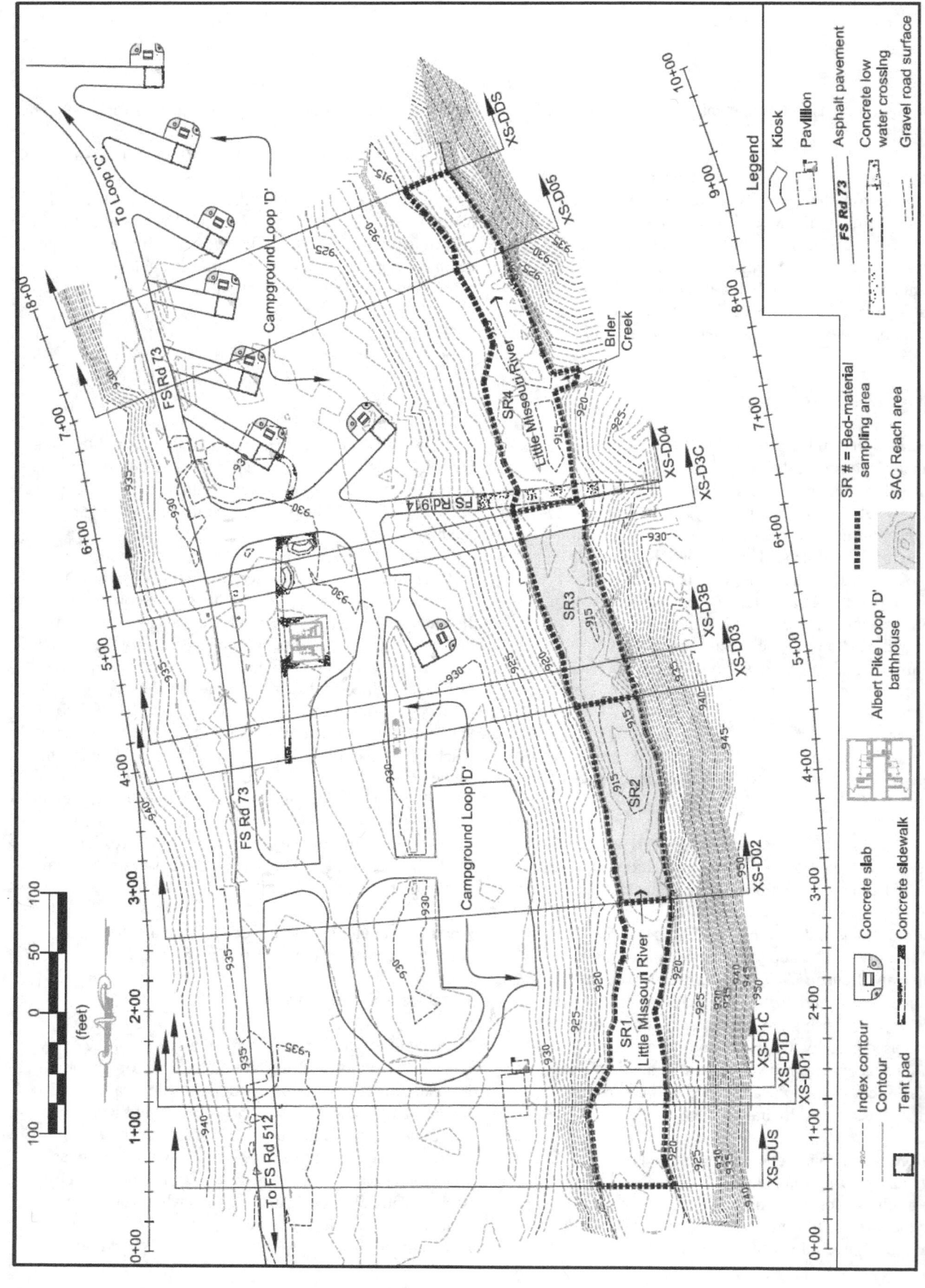

Figure 3—The combined Upper and Lower Loop D study reaches and associated baselines, cross sections, bed-material sampling areas, and campground developments in the Albert Pike Recreation Area. For clarity, the extent of the slope-area computation reach is only shown within the active channel.

buildings, and campsites) were surveyed to facilitate overlaying the campground development plans onto the topographic data. Elevation above mean sea level and geographic coordinates were established at selected points in both Loop C and D Campgrounds using global positioning equipment. These elevations and coordinates were then transferred to a set of additional control points within each study reach using a level survey. The control-points were used to establish the elevations and coordinates at all other survey points. Experienced survey professionals from the Ouachita and Ozark National Forests used electronic total stations and prism poles to accomplish the survey work.

Bed-material sizes were measured within the bankfull area of the LMR channel throughout all three study reaches to characterize grain-size distributions. Each study reach was divided into segments by visual inspection where substrate sizes appeared to change. In each segment, a 200-point Wolman pebble count was used to tally substrate grain size using standard size classes (Wolman 1954). Substrate was sampled by boot-tip using a zigzag pattern that repeatedly crossed the entire bankfull channel area (Bevenger and King 1995). Grain size was measured along the intermediate axis using a metric tape measure. A substantial portion of the bankfull channel is bedrock outcrops which occur not as horizontal slabs or beds, but as sculpted knobs or blocks protruding into the streamflow (fig. 10A). The contribution of bedrock to grain roughness was estimated by measuring the vertical distance that bedrock at a given sample location projected above the surrounding bed elevation and recording this as its grain size. Various substrate size metrics were later used to estimate Manning n roughness values within the bankfull channel area. Details on estimating roughness values are given below and in appendix A.

Channel Geometry Data Derivation

Cross sections were initially located where significant changes in main-channel roughness occurred. Additional cross sections were generated later in the analysis to enable more confident estimates of either peak discharge during the 11 June event or HWEs. Cross-sectional geometry data were derived from 1-foot contours generated from the survey data using AutoCAD. The geometry data were compiled as distance and elevation data pairs along the cross section. Boundaries between cover types were also plotted on the cross sections. Boundary locations were used to compute the ground distances for each cover type along each section.

Surface roughness values were characterized using Manning n values. Following the guidelines in Benson and Dalrymple

(1967) and Davidian (1984), each cross section was divided into subsections based on topography and cover-type changes. In most cases, only two subsections were needed: one for the main channel and one for the left overbank area. At the downstream end of the Loop C reach where the Loop B Campground is located, the right overbank area was sufficient in size that right-overbank subsections were also delineated in this portion of the Loop C reach. For each subsection, a procedure equivalent to the Modified Channel Method (Arcement and Schneider 1989) was used to estimate roughness values outside of the bankfull channel area. Manning n values were assigned to each cover type. For the bankfull channel area within each main-channel subsection, the roughness value was determined using the mean value from seven different empirical equations previously developed to estimate Manning n values (appendix A). For each subsection, the slope lengths of the bankfull channel or each cover type were summed and a weighted mean roughness value was computed. The weighted means were used as the initial estimates for Manning n values in each subsection and revised later based on the results of the discharge model selection process described below.

High-water elevations for the 11 June event were estimated for all cross sections using the numerous high-water marks that were located and surveyed on both sides of the LMR within the three study reaches. The methods of Benson and Dalrymple (1967) were followed in locating and selecting high-water marks. In addition, all high-water marks identified and marked by U.S. Geological Survey (USGS) personnel in the days immediately after the 11 June event that occurred in or near the three study reaches were surveyed as well.

The datasets used to predict the HWEs for all cross sections were compiled as follows. The locations and elevations of all marks were plotted on topographic maps (1 inch = 40 feet scale) produced using AutoCAD software. Two maps were plotted: one for the Loop C study reach and one for the combined Upper and Lower Loop D study reaches. Baselines were established on each map parallel to the approximate centerline of the low-flow channel of the LMR, and all high-water marks were projected perpendicularly onto these baselines. An arbitrary origin location was established on each baseline a short distance upstream from the upstream-most cross section, and the station distances of the high-water marks were measured relative to these origins. Station distance and elevation data were then compiled for each high-water mark.

Initial Discharge Modeling

To estimate the peak discharge of the 11 June event, a preliminary model was first computed in the Loop C and Upper Loop D study reaches. Computing the preliminary model accomplished two objectives. First, it identified a section of the study reach whose characteristics permit accurate discharge estimates to be made. Second, it identified a set of roughness values and HWEs to be used as a starting point in identifying potentially better models. How the preliminary model was used to accomplish the second objective is explained in the next section.

The preliminary model for the 11 June event was computed using the slope-area method (Dalrymple and Benson 1968, Herschy 1995). The slope-area method, based on the one-dimensional energy equation, assumes gradually varied, steady flow conditions for computing discharge. While discharge varies greatly over time and space during an entire flood event, these variations are typically considered to be small over the relatively short distance used to estimate discharge and the time duration during which peak discharge occurs; therefore, steady-flow conditions are commonly assumed for modeling purposes (Davidian 1984). The slope-area method is probably the most commonly used technique for estimating peak discharge when direct measurements of streamflow velocities are not available (Dalrymple and Benson 1984, Jarrett 1987, Rantz 1982).

The Slope-Area Computation (SAC) program (Fulford 1994) calculates discharge using the slope-area method, and was used to calculate all peak discharge estimates for the 11 June event. In addition to discharge, the SAC program computes the following hydraulic metrics or diagnostic terms, which are used to judge how well the model meets the assumptions of the slope-area method:

- Fall
- Spread
- Conveyance
- Velocity head
- Froude number
- Total friction head for multiple subreaches (HF)
- Ratio of the computed discharge divided by the discharge computed with no expansion loss (CX)
- Ratio of the velocity head change in a contracting channel section divided by the friction head (RC)
- Ratio of the velocity head change in an expanding channel section divided by the friction head (RX)
- Ratio of channel section length to maximum flow depth

Diagnostic terms were evaluated for the entire reach used to model discharge and for the subreaches which comprise the modeled reach. The whole-reach discharge was used as the final prediction for a given model.

To compute the peak discharge, only a portion of each study reach was used. The slope-area method is most accurate where channel conditions most closely match the criteria specified by Benson and Dalrymple (1967) and Dalrymple and Benson (1968). These criteria could not be met along the entire length of each study reach, but they could be met along shorter sections (hereafter called "SAC reaches"). Each SAC reach was the longest portion of the study reach which could be identified that best met the selection criteria. These selection criteria and a description of the SAC reaches characteristics are given in appendix C.

Two SAC reaches were used: one in the Upper Loop D reach and one in the Loop C reach (figs. 2 and 3). The discharge computed for each SAC reach can be confidently extrapolated to the larger respective study reaches because no tributaries, flow diversions, or storage areas occur that might significantly change discharge within those study reaches. In the case of the Lower Loop D reach, the discharge computed for the SAC reach in Loop C is used because discharge is assumed not to change between the confluence of Brier Creek and the downstream end of the Loop C reach.

Candidate Model Identification

The preliminary slope-area model has a set of roughness values and HWEs associated with each of the cross sections used in the calculations. Both the roughness values and HWEs are subject to uncertainty because both are estimated using a combination of field observations and model predictions. While the procedures used to determine the roughness values and HWEs for computing the preliminary model are assumed to produce good estimates, it is possible that the actual roughness values or HWEs differ somewhat from the initial estimates. If so, then more accurate slope-area models might be identified by varying the roughness values or HWEs from the initial estimates. This was done for roughness values only because their estimation is more subjective.

Alternative slope-area models were identified by systematically varying roughness values, recomputing the model, and selecting those models that produced hydraulic metrics better than those produced by the preliminary model. The roughness values for the preliminary model were used to determine the range of roughness values that were tested. It was assumed that actual roughness values for each subsection might differ by as much as ±10 percent from the largest initial value among the three cross sections. Given this assumption, a range of n values from -0.008 to +0.008 of the initial estimate for each subsection was tested using increments of ±0.002. The increment was applied to all subsections of the same type (e.g., the left-overbank subsections) for all three cross sections in the SAC reach, the model recomputed, and the results saved. All permutations of the varied roughness values were computed. The hydraulic metrics for all models were inspected and a subset of two to three candidate models were identified whose hydraulic metrics indicated they were better than the preliminary model. Further details on the candidate models considered and the criteria used to identify these models are given in appendix D.

Best Model Selection

The final step in judging the candidate slope-area models was to assess how well the computed HWEs for each of the candidate models compared to the observed HWEs. In this step, HWEs were computed for *all* cross sections within the study reach based on the discharge and roughness value changes associated with each candidate model. For cross sections outside the SAC reaches, the same differences in roughness values used to compute the candidate model were applied to the appropriate subsections. For example, if the candidate model used a change of -0.004 from the initial roughness estimate for the left-overbank subsections, then the initial roughness values for left-overbank subsections in all the cross sections outside the SAC reach were changed (decreased, in this case) by that amount. Each incremental change was applied to all subsections because I think this method is more objective than applying individual changes to individual subsections. Because the methods used to estimate roughness values are the same for all subsections, then any error between actual and estimated roughness likely would occur consistently with all subsections of the same type, and not just in a single subsection of that type. Applying n value changes to specific subsections implies that some significant difference in cover characteristics must occur in these subsections; however, if this is true, then such changes should be accounted for in the adjustments made to the base n values for each cover type within each subsection (appendix A).

The standard-step (also known as the step-backwater) method (Brunner 2010b) was used to compute HWEs given the discharge, location, geometry, and roughness characteristics of all cross sections in the study reach. The standard-step method is a one-dimensional analysis that assumes gradually varied, steady flow conditions, the same assumptions used for the slope-area method (see above for the rationale for this assumption). The analysis approach used for this study assumes subcritical flows in calculating all HWEs, an assumption that was tested and confirmed as part of the analysis. The analysis process begins at the downstream-most cross section in a study reach and moves upstream, computing the HWE at each subsequent cross section through iteration. The same discharge is used for all cross sections in a study reach. The Hydrologic Engineering Center River Analysis System (HEC-RAS) program (Brunner 2010a) was used to compute HWEs for all cross sections.

To compare how well the computed HWEs matched the observed HWEs, each candidate model was evaluated using the following process:

1. An assumed HWE at the downstream-most cross section is specified as a boundary condition.
2. HWEs at all upstream cross sections in the reach are computed.
3. The difference between the observed HWE and the computed HWE is calculated for each cross section.
4. Based on the results of Step 3, a new HWE is specified at the downstream-most cross section, and Steps 2 and 3 are repeated.

The process was repeated until the overall differences computed in Step 3 for all cross sections in the study reach were minimized. The first HWE used in Step 1 was the average of the observed HWEs for the left- and right-banks at the downstream-most cross section. The new HWE used in Step 4 was not allowed to be greater than the maximum or less than the minimum of the left- and right-bank HWEs at the downstream-most cross section.

Finally, the best peak-discharge model was determined by considering all three sets of evaluation measures: (1) the hydraulic diagnostic values for the model in the SAC reach, (2) the discharge differences between subreaches within the SAC reach, and (3) how well the computed HWEs match the observed HWEs within the entire study reach. The chosen model was the one whose characteristics provided the optimal combination of the evaluation measures. The chosen model provided both the best estimate of peak discharge for the 11 June event and the roughness values associated with all cross sections in the study reach.

Sensitivity Analysis

A sensitivity analysis of the selected slope-area models for the Loop C and Upper Loop D SAC reaches was done to assess how estimated discharge and model quality changed when both roughness values and head drop were varied. The range of Manning n values was ±0.004 from the final subsection n values for the selected model, using increments of ±0.002. Head drop was varied using the range for the left- and right-bank HWEs estimated for the SAC reach cross sections. Both a maximum and a minimum head-drop case were examined. The maximum head-drop case used the higher of the estimated left- and right-bank HWEs for the upstream-most cross section, and the lower HWE of the two estimates for the downstream-most cross section. The minimum case used the lower HWE and higher HWE for the upstream and downstream cross sections, respectively. In both cases, the HWE for the middle cross section was left unchanged from that used in the final model. The permutations of these changes produced 50 models that were computed for each SAC reach and compared to their respective final models to assess how much model outputs were affected by varying these key parameters.

Computing Other Flood Discharges

To compute the HWEs for floods other than the 11 June event, it is necessary to first determine their peak discharges. The National Research Council (2009) identifies three general methods for determining peak discharges for flood mapping studies: (1) flood-frequency models derived from streamflow gauging data, (2) rainfall-runoff models, and (3) regional-regression models.

The nearest gaging station to the APRA on the LMR is the USGS Langley station (station number 07360200) which is located approximately 10 miles downstream of the APRA. Drainage area at the Langley station is approximately twice that at the APRA. This size difference precluded using the Langley station data to directly represent streamflow characteristics at the APRA. At present, no rainfall-runoff model is available that is applicable to the upper LMR basin. Therefore, a set of regression equations derived from a regional flood-frequency analysis by Hodge and Tasker (1995) was used to estimate the peak discharges for the 10-, 25-, 50-, and 100-year floods at both the Upper Loop D and Loop C study reaches. USGS regional-regression models such as those used in this study have been found to estimate flood discharges with sufficient precision to support Federal Emergency Management Agency flood mapping efforts nationwide (National Research Council 2009).

The regression equations use three basin characteristics to estimate peak discharge in the hydrologic region containing the upper LMR basin: (1) drainage area, (2) mean basin elevation, and (3) basin shape factor (Hodge and Tasker 1995). The measurements needed to either determine or compute these variables were obtained using ArcGIS and spatial datasets managed by the Ouachita National Forest. Measurements for the Upper Loop D reach used the confluence with Brier Creek as the basin outlet; those for the Loop C reach used the FS Rd 106 bridge location (fig. 1). While both drainage area and basin shape were determined using the procedures described in U.S. Geological Survey (1998), mean basin elevation was determined using approximately 780,000-880,000 digital elevation model points within the respective catchments instead of the approximately 50 regularly spaced grid points specified by the U.S. Geological Survey (1998). This difference in method was used merely for convenience and should not affect the accuracy of the regression predictions.

Two variations on the regional-regression method were also considered. The weighted-estimate method uses data from a gaging station in the same drainage basin to adjust the peak-discharge predictions obtained from the regional-regression models (U.S. Geological Survey 1998). Data from the Langley station (water years 1989-2009) is available to apply this method, and was used to compute weighted discharge estimates following the method described in Hodge and Tasker (1995) but updated by the U.S. Geological Survey (1998). However, the weighting method is not recommended when the drainage area for the ungauged site is less than 50 percent of that for the gauged site. The drainage area for the Langley station is 68.2 square miles, while the drainage area for the downstream most study reach (Loop C) is 34.0 square miles, thus none of the study reaches have drainages that exceed the 50-percent guideline. Nonetheless, the weighted-estimates were computed for the Loop C study reach because this reach was close to the minimum size, and so that predictions from the two methods could be compared. A log-Pearson Type III model was used to predict the peak discharges at the Langley station based on the observed data series. The other variation of the regional-regression method is the region-of-influence regression method (Hodge and Tasker 1995). The region-of-influence regression method was not used for this study because the method is still under development and the USGS considers it secondary to the regional-regression method (U.S. Geological Survey 1998).

Computing Other Flood Elevations

A standard step analysis was also used to compute the HWEs for the 10-, 25-, 50-, and 100-year peak discharges. This one-dimensional modeling of HWEs produces accurate results for flood mapping (Buchele and others 2006), especially in situations such as those at the APRA where multiple flow paths, in-channel structures (e.g., culverts or bridges), and significant lateral inflows do not occur or can be excluded from the modeled area. The analysis uses the peak discharge estimated for a given flood, along with the cross-section location, geometry, and roughness characteristics associated with the best discharge model. The analysis assumes that the cross-section geometry and roughness values for any future flood will be the same as those which occurred during the 11 June flood. The analysis uses the same assumptions and computation procedures as those used to select the best discharge model for the 11 June event with one exception: a different boundary condition is required because the HWE at the downstream-most cross section is not known for any event other than the 11 June flood. For this analysis, the normal depth at the downstream-most cross section is used. The normal depth is computed using the energy gradient calculated for the HWEs of the 11 June event at the same cross section. This energy gradient is assumed to be constant for all floods. The HEC-RAS model is again used to compute all cross-section HWEs in each study reach. The HEC-RAS application meets the Federal Emergency Management Agency's requirements for flood hazard analysis (Federal Emergency Management Agency 2010a), and has been widely used in studies required by the National Flood Insurance Program (Federal Emergency Management Agency 2010b) for computing HWEs for events such as the 100-year flood.

RESULTS AND DISCUSSION

Reach Characteristics

Cross-section shapes were generally consistent within each study reach. Cross-section plots for the Loop C study reach are shown in figure 4 while those for the Upper and Lower Loop D study reaches are shown in figure 5. There is a continuous terrace along the left bank of all three study reaches. In the Loop C reach, this left-bank terrace is approximately 150-200 feet wide. In the Upper and Lower Loop D reaches, the terrace width is approximately 200-300 feet. Both the Loop C and Loop D Campgrounds are located on the left-bank terrace (figs. 2 and 3). The main channel is a single-thread channel throughout the Albert Pike Recreation Area (APRA), and is incised approximately

10-15 feet below the left-bank terrace level. The main channel is bounded by a continuous hillslope along the right bank except where Brier Creek joins the Little Missouri River (LMR) midway between XS-D04 and XS-D05 (fig. 3) and at the downstream end of the Loop C reach (fig. 2). The valley width constricts somewhat starting at the Brier Creek confluence and continuing downstream into the Loop C reach. This can be seen by comparing cross sections at and upstream of XS-D04 with those downstream until XS-C02 (figs. 4 and 5). Starting at XS-C03, a higher and smaller terrace occurs on the right bank and extends past XS-C05. This right-bank terrace is about 50-100 feet wide, and is the location of the Loop B Campground (figs. 2 and 4).

Four segments with differing roughness characteristics occur within the main-channel areas of the Loop C study reach (shown as SR1 to SR4 in fig. 2) and the combined Upper and Lower Loop D study reaches (shown as SR1 to SR4 in fig. 3). Substrate size distributions for the Loop C segments are shown in figure 6, while those in the Upper and Lower Loop D study reach are shown in figure 7. The mobile bed material is predominantly coarse gravel to large cobble in size (1.3-10 inches [32-256 mm]) in all of the segments. Bedrock makes up 19-30 percent of the bed material in all segments except that between XS-C02 to XS-C03, where it is 40 percent. No evidence of significant scour or fill from the 11 June event was evident in any of the main-channel segments, although noticeable scour was reported by local residents 800 feet downstream of XS-C05 in a meander-bend pool used as a swimming hole (Holmes and Wagner 2011). Furthermore, there are no knickpoints or other features in any of the three study reaches that would produce a free overfall condition in the main channel. The occurrence of either scour/fill or a free overfall would reduce the accuracy of the slope-area and standard step analysis results.

The Upper and Lower Loop D reaches classify as B4c- and B4c stream types, respectively, using the Rosgen (1996) classification system, while the Loop C reach classifies as a C4c- upstream of XS-C03 and a C3c- downstream (table 1). The "c" and "c-" designations are used because the water-surface slopes are less than 0.02 and 0.001, respectively. For the most part, the study reaches or sections of the reaches exhibit morphological characteristics that fall within the ranges reported by Rosgen (1996) for these stream types. The consistent exception is for sinuosity, which is extremely low throughout the APRA and below the ranges reported by Rosgen (1996). Also, the entrenchment ratio for Loop C upstream of XS-C03 is below that reported by Rosgen (1996) for C4 stream types. The substantial amount of bedrock in the channel, which constrains its ability to

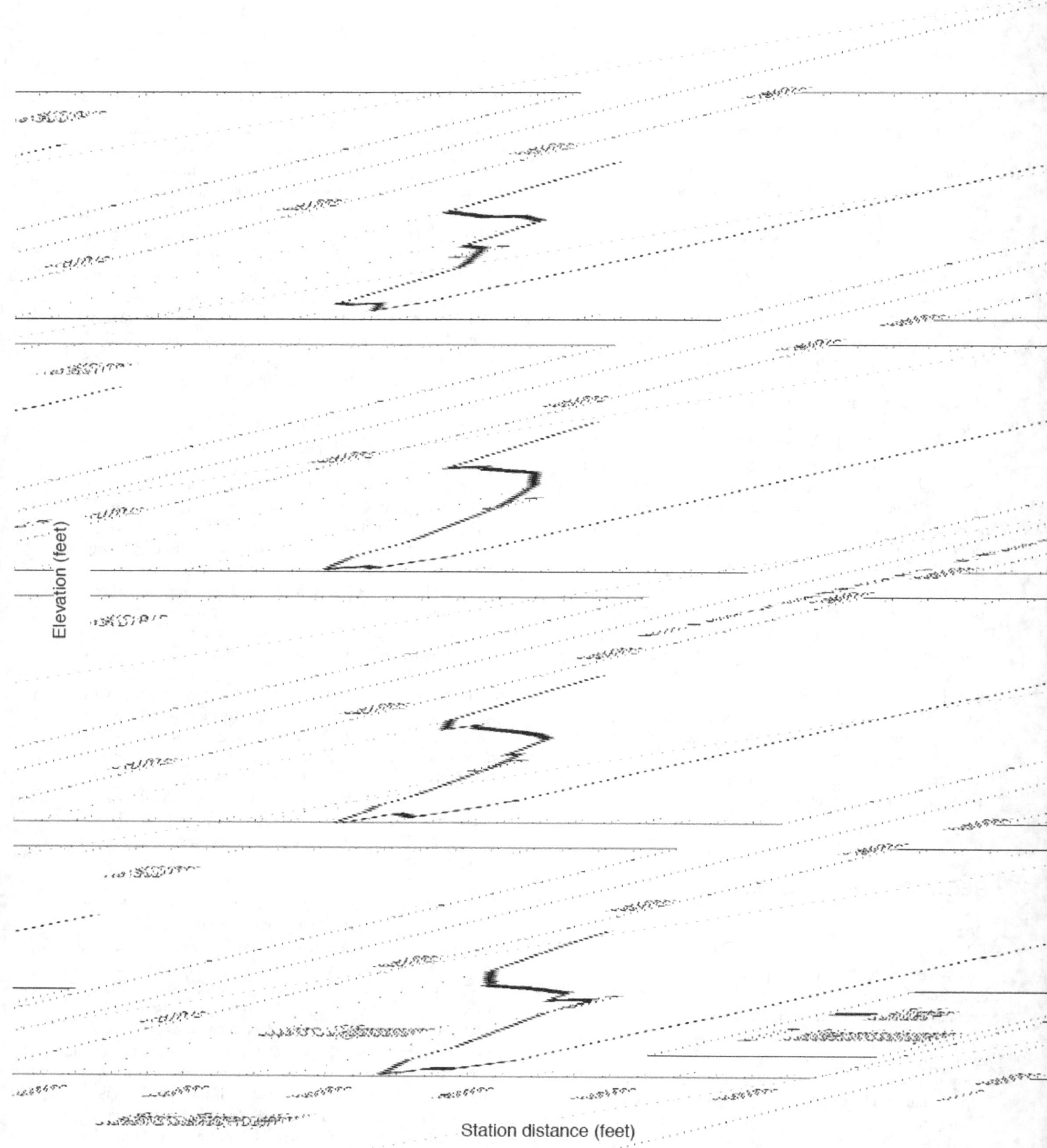

Figure 4   Cross-section plots for Loop C study reach in the Albert Pike Recreation Area View is looking downstream Vertical dotted lines indicate the horizontal position of the Loops B and C campgrounds within each cross section (continued)

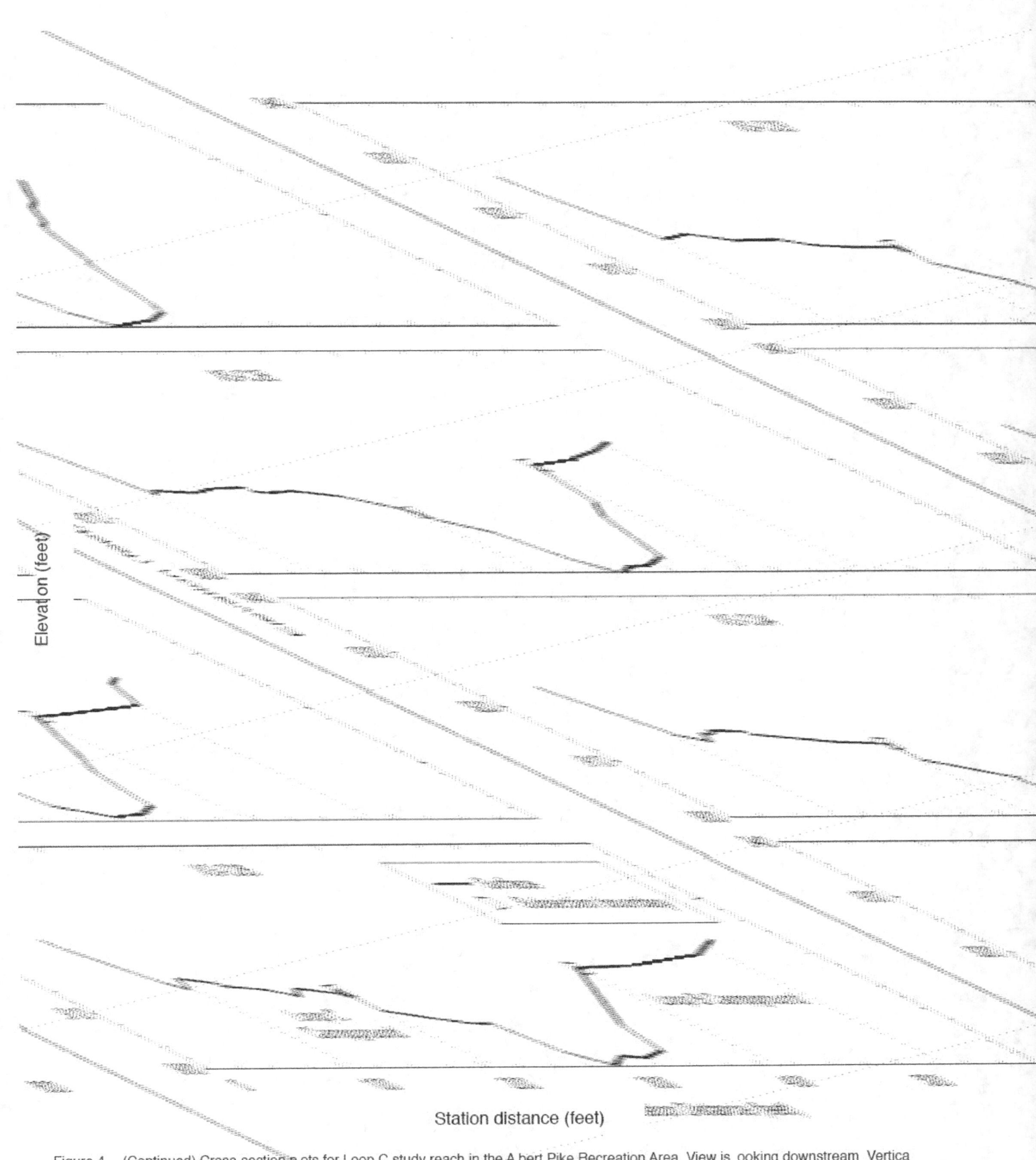

Figure 4   (Continued) Cross-section plots for Loop C study reach in the Albert Pike Recreation Area. View is looking downstream. Vertical dotted lines indicate the horizontal position of the Loops B and C campgrounds within each cross section.

Figure 5   Cross-section plots for Upper and Lower Loop D study reaches in the Albert Pike Recreation Area   View is looking downstream   Vertical dotted lines indicate the horizontal position of the Loop D campground within each cross section   (continued)

Elevation (feet)

Station distance (feet)

14

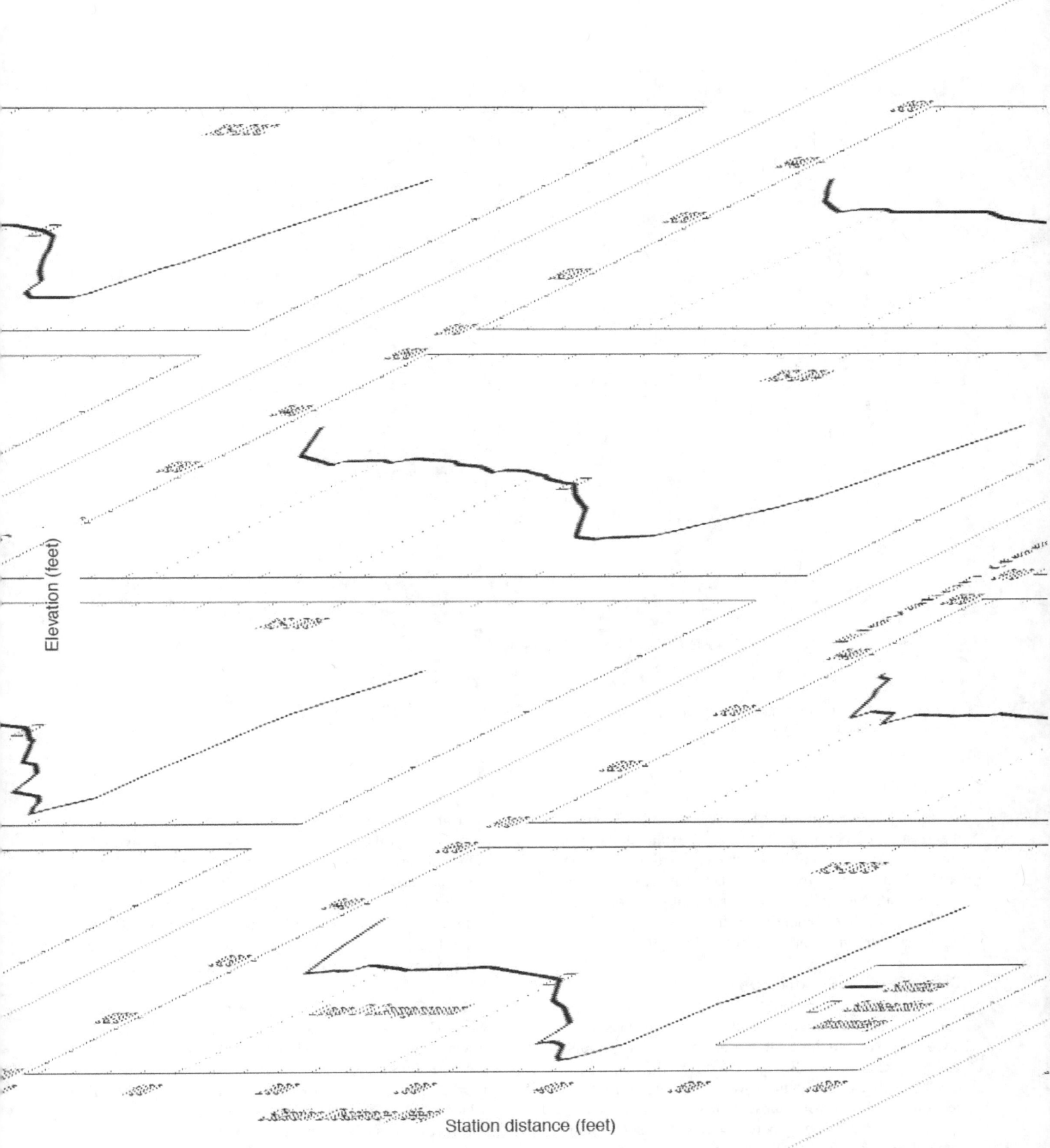

Figure 5   (Continued) Cross-section p ots for Upper and Lower Loop D study reaches in the A bert Pike Recreation Area View is ooking downstream Vertica dotted ines indicate the horizonta position of the Loop D campground within each cross section

15

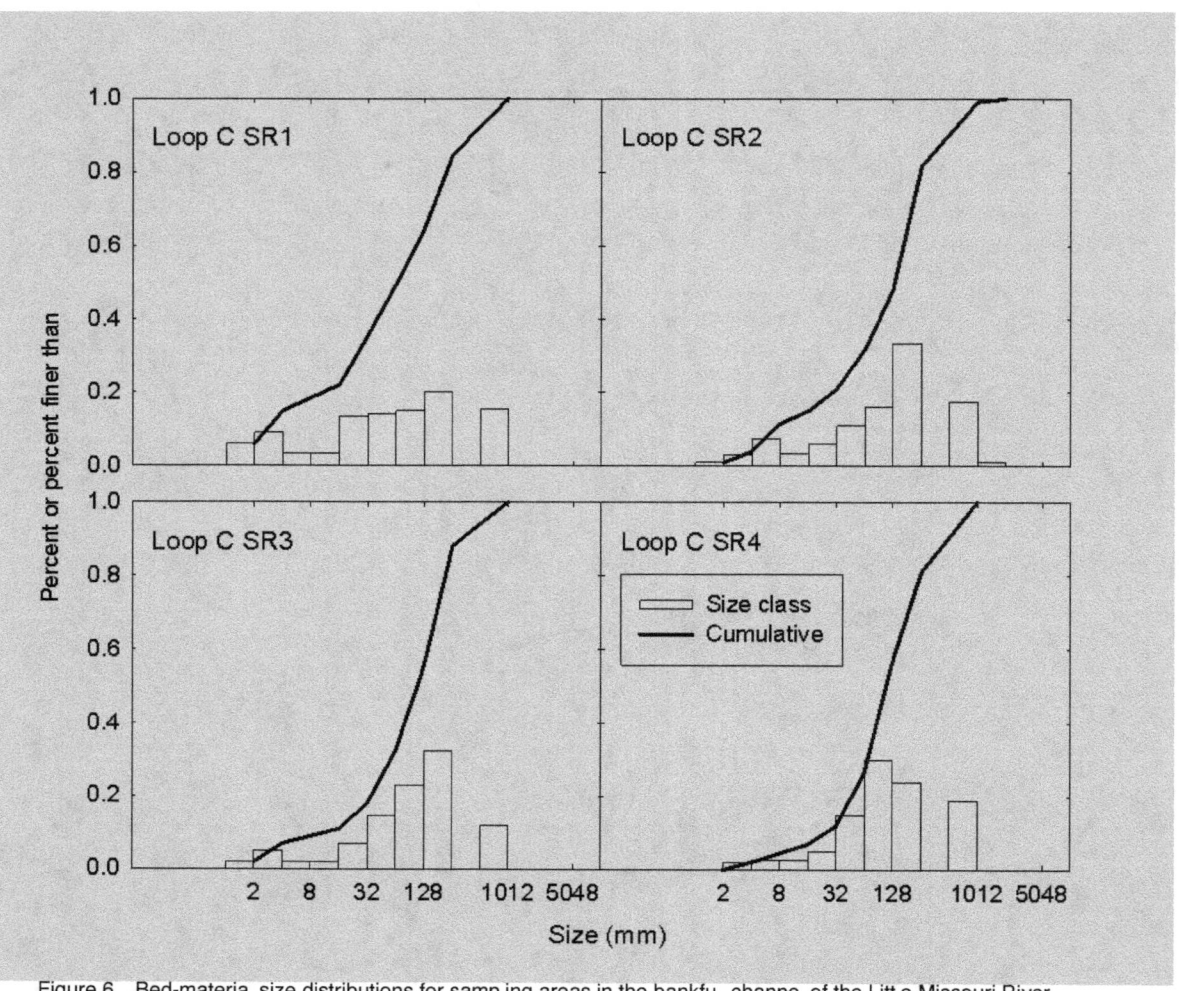

Figure 6 Bed-materia size distributions for samp ing areas in the bankfu channe of the Litt e Missouri River in the Loop C study reach

downcut, may account for the low water-surface slopes that occur. Bedrock would not seem to explain the low sinuosities as there is little bedrock exposed in the channel banks. A more likely explanation is that most streams in the Ouachita Mountains follow structural joints or faults occurring within the underlying strata, and these joints are often quite straight over distances of 1,000 feet or more.

Cross-Section Subdivision

For analysis, all cross sections in the study reaches were divided into two to three subsections based on topography and cover changes. In the Upper and Lower Loop D study reaches, only two subsections were used for all cross sections: a left-overbank subsection and a main-channel subsection. The boundary between these two subsections generally corresponds to the abrupt cover type change from the forest cover along the main channel (fig. 10A) to the open cover types associated with the campground developments (fig. 10C). This cover-type change occurs at

or near the marked slope break where the relatively steep upper bank of the main channel ends and the relatively flat left-bank terrace begins (figs. 4 and 5). The right side of all main-channel subsections in the two Loop D study reaches was extended to the cross-section end. This approach, in contrast to breaking out a hillslope subsection on the right bank, has been shown to produce more accurate estimates of roughness values for the entire subsection (Davidian 1984).

In Loop C, all cross sections upstream of and including XS-C03 were divided into two subsections, while those downstream were divided into three (fig. 4). The upstream cross sections are similar to those in the Loop D study reaches, having left-overbank and main-channel subsections which are divided at or near the slope break where the forest cover near the channel ends and the more open cover types of the campground area begins. For the cross sections downstream of XS-C03, a right-overbank subsection is broken out where the right-bank terrace area occurs. As with the left-overbank, the boundary between the right-overbank

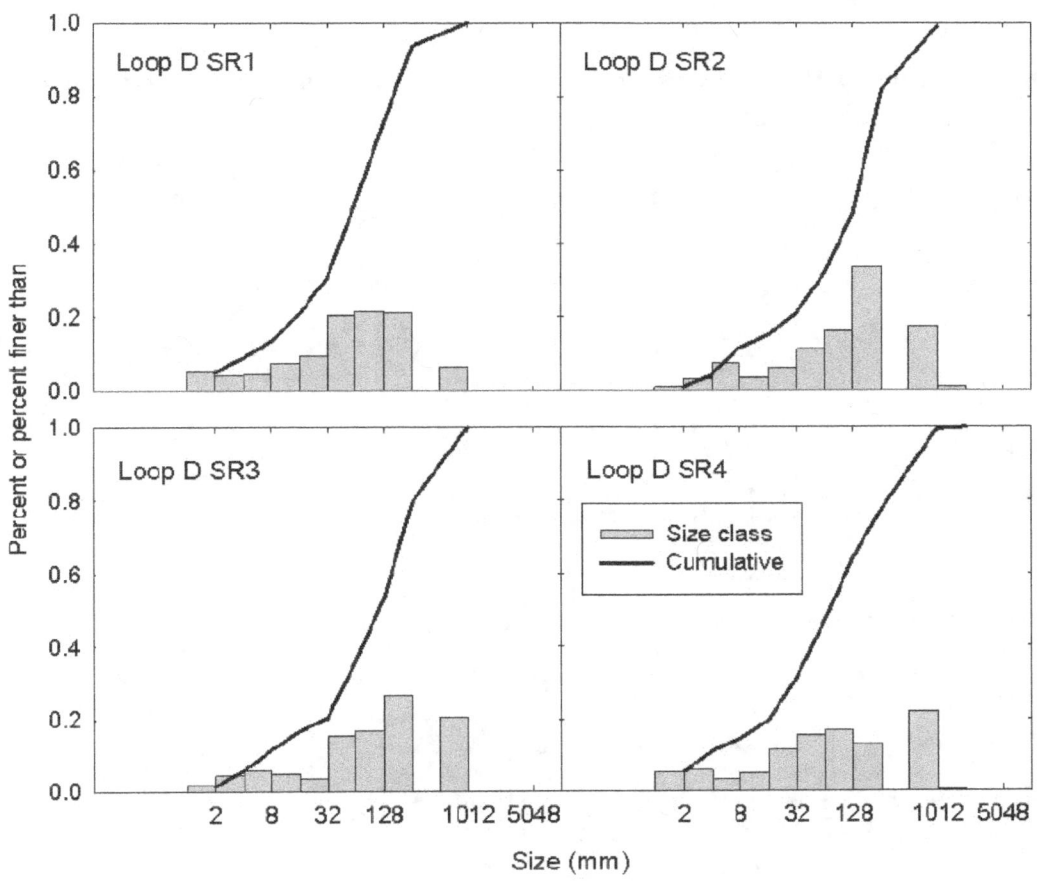

Figure 7   Bed-material size distributions for sampling areas in the bankfull channel of the Little Missouri River in the Upper and Lower Loop D study reaches

and main-channel subsections is the abrupt slope break and cover type change from forest to open campground.

The decision to subdivide the cross sections is justified based on the criteria given in Davidian (1984—attributed separately to Tice and Matthai). The criteria were confirmed using cross-section dimensions derived from both the 11 June event and the 10-year flood (table 2). Only ratios for left-overbank subsections are given in table 2, as all potential right-overbank subsections (cross sections XS-C03 to XS-C05) have ratios that are greater than those for the corresponding left-overbank subsections. This occurs because elevations are higher in the right-overbank subsections, thus flow depths are always shallower. The ratio of top width to subsection flow depth is greater than 5 (Tice criteria) for all cross sections at both flood levels (table 2). The ratio of maximum cross-section flow depth to maximum subsection flow depth is greater than 2 (Matthai) for all cross sections at the 10-year flood level, and all but four cross sections at the 11 June flood level. Three of

these cross sections occur at the upstream end of the Loop C study reach (XS-CUS, XS-C01, and XS-C1B) while the remaining one (XS-C3B) occurs in the middle of the reach. The case of XS-C3B is borderline (Matthai ratio = 1.94) and since it occurs between two cross sections which meet both guidelines, XS-C3B was also subdivided to avoid undesirable hydraulic changes (Davidian 1984). Given the need to subdivide all other cross sections in the Loop C reach, the three cross sections at the upstream end were also subdivided to produce the best representation of a uniform reach. As cross-section subdivision is justified for both the 10-year and 11 June floods, then it follows that it is also justified for all intermediate flood levels, too.

11 June Flood Discharge

High-water elevations—The observed elevations for high-water marks in the Loop C and combined Loop D study reaches are plotted in figure 8. Almost all marks were wash lines created by fine organic debris or sediment on

Table 1—Morphological data used to classify the Albert Pike Recreation Area study reaches using the Rosgen (1996) system

Channel section	Entrenchment ratio	Width-to-depth ratio	Sinuosity	Water-surface slope	Bed material D_{50} size class	Rosgen stream type
Upper Loop D reach	1.4-1.8	17-22	<1.1 [a]	<0.001	Coarse to very coarse gravel	B4c-
Lower Loop D reach	1.9-2.0	19	<1.1 [a]	0.005	Coarse to very coarse gravel	B4c
Loop C reach upstream of XS-C03	2.0-2.5 [a]	17-19	<1.1 [a]	<0.001	Coarse to very coarse gravel	C4c-
Loop C reach downstream of XS-C03	2.0-2.7	19-20	<1.1 [a]	<0.001	Cobble	C3c-

[a] Va ues are be ow the range reported by Rosgen (1996) for these stream types

Table 2— Tice and Matthai ratios (Davidian 1984) and width-to-depth ratios for cross sections in the Albert Pike Recreation Area study reaches based on high-water elevations during the 10-year and June 11, 2010, floods. Tice and Matthai ratios are computed for left-overbank subsections only

Study reach	Cross section	10-year flood			11 June flood		
		Tice[a]	Matthai[b]	Width / depth[c]	Tice[a]	Matthai[b]	Width / depth[c]
Loop C	XS-CUS	17.91	2.36	7.59	11.44	1.78	6.43
	XS-C01	19.46	2.44	7.99	12.83	1.83	6.99
	XS-C1B	18.64	2.16	8.63	12.84	1.72	7.45
	XS-C02	27.95	3.23	8.65	16.75	2.15	7.80
	XS-C03	40.07	4.39	9.12	19.17	2.50	7.67
	XS-C3B	25.30	2.65	9.54	15.42	1.94	7.96
	XS-C04	34.81	3.92	8.88	17.55	2.32	7.56
	XS-C05	44.91	6.14	7.32	17.77	2.77	6.42
Upper Loop D	XS-DUS	69.08	6.61	10.45	40.72	3.12	13.06
	XS-D01	48.64	4.15	11.71	37.84	2.56	14.76
	XS-D1D	49.91	4.33	11.53	37.06	2.57	14.43
	XS-D1C	51.16	4.56	11.23	37.20	2.62	14.19
	XS-D02	60.04	5.78	10.38	39.29	2.87	13.71
	XS-D03	49.20	4.33	11.35	37.19	2.62	14.17
	XS-D3B	48.64	4.02	12.10	34.99	2.48	14.11
	XS-D3C	58.40	3.99	14.63	31.88	2.41	13.25
	XS-D04	46.52	2.93	15.87	27.48	2.04	13.49
Lower Loop D	XS-D05	63.85	5.92	10.78	26.54	2.84	9.36
	XS-DDS	72.76	6.26	11.63	27.15	2.85	9.52

Note: Since the description of the ratios in Davidian (1984) does not make c ear how flow depths are determined the maximun depths or the respective subsections are used because these produce the owest (most conservative) ratios
[a] Tice ratio = cross section top width/overbank subsection depth
[b] Matthai ratio = maximum cross section depth/overbank subsection depth The main-channe subsection a ways has the maximum cross-section depth
[c] Width/depth = cross section top width/maximum cross section depth

the ground surface; however, six marks in Loop C and two marks in the combined Loop D reaches were sediment or seed lines on tree trunks that were identified and marked by U.S. Geological Survey (USGS) personnel. Confidence in the accuracy of all marks was judged fair to excellent. No significant rainfall occurred between June 11 and the last half of July when all non-USGS marks were flagged, and none occurred prior to the marks being surveyed in early August. During the field survey of the Loop C reach, 19 and 15 high-water marks were identified and mapped along the left and right banks, respectively. For the combined Loop D reaches, 24 and 25 marks were mapped along the left and right banks. The upstream-most mark on the left bank was approximately 150 feet outside of the Upper Loop D study reach, but was included because it was an excellent high-water mark. Of the total number mapped, four marks on the right bank of the Loop C reach and two marks on the right bank of the combined Loop D reaches were deemed suspect and excluded from further analysis. See appendix B for further discussion of the excluded high-water mark data.

To model the vertical variation in high-water elevation (HWE) with distance along each bank, a running-median smooth with a five-element window was used (fig. 8). The elevations of the high-water marks along the distance axis suggest that a simple linear model would not accurately capture the trend along an entire bank for three of the four banks (the right bank of the combined Loop D reaches being the possible exception). A running-median was used because it retains more of the variation over short distances while smoothing out abrupt changes produced by single observations.

The observed high-water marks also suggested that HWEs differed between the left and right banks in all three study reaches. This difference between banks is most evident in the combined Loop D reaches where there is almost no overlap of HWEs between the two banks except along the first 100 feet of the Upper Loop D reach (fig. 8A). In the Loop C reach (fig. 8B), the HWEs are intermixed between banks, but there are sections of the reach where clear differences are observed (e.g., the downstream third). Because of the differences between left- and right-banks, separate trend models were computed for each bank in each reach. Using the separate models, fitted values were computed for each observed high-water mark along each left and right bank (fig. 8).

The valley constriction starting at the Brier Creek confluence did not appear to create a backwater effect during the 11 June flood. The HWEs immediately upstream of the confluence (fig. 8A) do not indicate a sharp

flattening in the general water-surface profile upstream of the confluence. Moreover, no significant flood deposits were observed immediately upstream of the Brier Creek confluence, especially along the right bank where Brier Creek joins the LMR, that might suggest a drop in flow velocity within the LMR due to a damming effect produced by Brier Creek streamflow during the 11 June flood.

The HWEs estimated for each cross section are listed in table 3. These estimates were computed using linear interpolation between the fitted values computed for the observed data. The differences between the left- and right-bank HWEs for each cross section were generally less than 1.00 foot, as shown in the Range column in table 3. These differences do not seem unusual given the relatively high variation in surface roughness within the reaches and that streamflow widths were 300-500 feet. HWE data reported by Mastin and Kresch (2005) also show marked variation between left and right banks, even for marks rated good to excellent. However, Mastin and Kresch's marks were surveyed 9 months after the flood occurred and were on a much larger river with a higher peak discharge.

Initial roughness values—Initial estimates for Manning n values show clear differences in roughness between the main-channel and the overbank subsections in all three study reaches. The initial roughness estimates are listed in table 4 for all cross sections. The differences between the main-channel and overbank subsections are not surprising given the cover changes created by construction of the campground facilities. The main-channel subsections are composed of a coarse gravel to large cobble size substrate in the channel bed, and generally have dense shrub or forest vegetation along the upper banks (figs. 10A and 10D). In contrast, the over-bank subsections generally have a mixture of patchy forest, or pavement and grass cover with scattered trees (figs. 10B and 10C).

The initial estimates of Manning n values seem reasonable when compared to computed n values for other sites with similar bed material and cover type characteristics. Sites with n values between 0.055 and 0.075 were identified using the USGS "n-Values Project" Web site (Soong and others, no date). Those with bed material sizes and bank cover similar to main-channel subsections within the LMR study reaches are listed in table 5. Only n values for the main-channel subsections can be compared because main-channel n values are the only ones available from this source. The assumption that the roughness values determined for the 11 June event are the same that occur for the other high-flow events considered in this analysis (i.e., that past a certain flow depth roughness remains constant despite

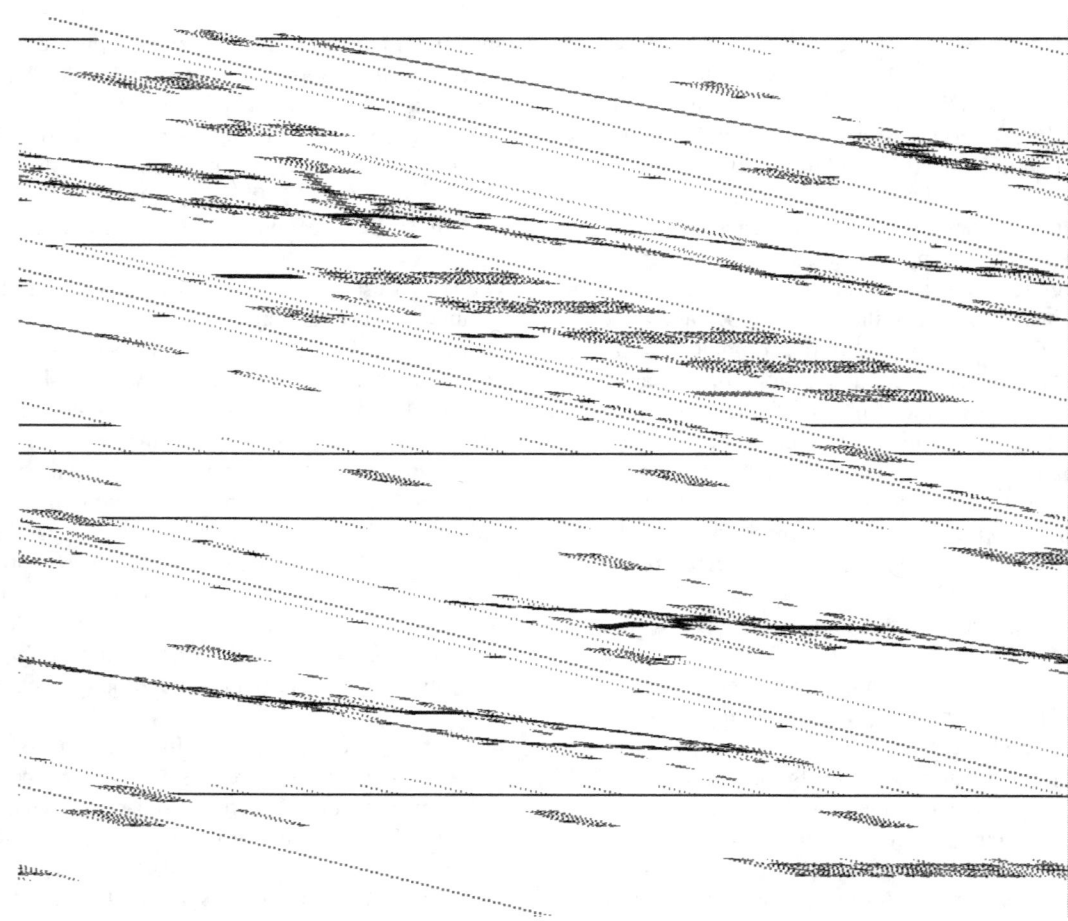

Figure 8   P ot of observed and smoothed high-water e evations produced by the June 11 2010 flood in the combined Loop D and Loop C study reaches The indicated cross sections in each p ot mark the upstream and downstream boundaries of the channe area used to estimate peak discharge for the flood in the Upper Loop D and Loop C study reaches Cross-section ine engths are extended beyond the smooth high-water e evation curves to improve egibi ity and do not indicate cross-section ocations beyond the curves

further increase in flow depth) is well supported by the results. The rationale for making this assumption and the criteria for testing it are given in Benson and Dalrymple (1967). The first criterion specifies that the ratio of flow depth to roughness element size must be greater than 5 to assume constant roughness. This criterion was confirmed for all cross sections in all three study reaches (table 6). The criterion was tested using the bed material D_{90} size from the main-channel subsections as the roughness element size. The flow depth used was that needed to overspill the banks and inundate the overbank areas of each cross section. This flow depth is obviously less than that for the 11 June event, and was later determined to also be less than that for the lowest discharge considered in this study (the 10-year flood). The computed values all exceed the ratio value of 5, with ratios ranging from just over 5.04 to 7.34 (table 6). The second criterion is that flow width is much greater than flow depth. Width-to-depth ratios for the 10-year and 11 June

floods are all greater than 6.42 (table 2). Together, these results indicate that roughness values do remain constant within the flood discharge range considered here.

Loop C peak discharge—The 40,800-cubic feet per second model was selected as the best discharge model for the Loop C and Lower Loop D study reaches. The Slope Area Computation (SAC) reach defined by cross sections XS-C02, XS-C03, and XS-C04 (fig. 2) was used to estimate discharge. The SAC model diagnostics for the 40,800-cubic feet per second model (table 7) are as good as or better than all other models considered, and are generally quite good based on the evaluation criteria provided in Dalrymple and Benson (1968), Fulford (1994), and Kirby (1987). Fall values exceed the recommended minimum of 0.5 foot for both subreaches. The spread and *CX* parameters are 0 and 1.00 for both subreaches, respectively, which are optimal. Both subreaches exhibit downstream contraction and have *RC* values close to 0. Froude numbers for all subsections and entire cross sections are well below 1.0 indicating subcritical flow. Conveyance ratios are within the recommended range of 0.80-1.25. Subreach velocity heads are somewhat larger than fall values (ratios > 1), but not greatly so, and the reach ratio is less than 1, which is preferred. Friction heads are less than fall values as indicated by their ratios, which also is a desired condition. The stream length-to-depth ratios are well below the recommended value of 75, but this is the only model-quality criterion which is significantly violated. It is doubtful this particular criterion would be met in most cases for mountain streams like the LMR, where high morphologic complexity generally precludes long stretches of consistent hydraulic conditions. I judge both the failure to meet this particular criterion and the somewhat higher than desired velocity heads as relatively minor flaws that do not significantly decrease the accuracy of the 40,800-cubic feet per second model.

The computed HWEs for the 40,800-cubic feet per second model compare well with HWEs estimated using the observed high-water marks in Loop C (fig. 9B). Based on the standard step analysis using a 40,800-cubic feet per second discharge and associated roughness values from the SAC model, the computed HWEs for five of the eight cross sections were within the observed HWE range for their respective left and right banks, and one was less than 0.1 foot outside of the HWE range. The other two cross sections were less than 0.5 foot outside the observed HWE range. The fit of the computed HWEs to observed HWEs was as good as or better than all other models that were considered. This fit was also accomplished without applying arbitrary changes to roughness values at individual cross sections.

The average flow velocity in the left-overbank subsection of XS-C01 just upstream of the bathhouse (fig. 2) was near the 9 feet per second value that Holmes and Wagner

Table 3—High-water elevations estimated for cross sections in the Albert Pike Recreation Area study reaches

| | | | ----------------------- High-water elevation ----------------------- | | | |
Study reach	Cross section	Distance downstream[a]	Left-bank	Right-bank	Average	Range
			-- feet --			
Loop C	XS-CUS	155	924.93	925.31	925.12	0.38
	XS-C01	283	924.92	925.11	925.01	0.19
	XS-C1B	425	924.82	924.24	924.53	0.58
	XS-C02	451	924.78	924.18	924.48	0.60
	XS-C03	615	922.83	922.86	922.84	0.03
	XS-C3B	742	922.47	921.52	922.00	0.95
	XS-C04	846 817	922.32	921.42	921.87	0.90
	XS-C05	947 906	921.82	921.36	921.59	0.46
Upper Loop D	XS-DUS	53	938.57	939.08	938.82	0.51
	XS-D01	120	937.92	938.92	938.42	1.00
	XS-D1C	150	937.79	938.87	938.33	1.08
	XS-D02	258 297	937.16	938.50	937.83	1.34
	XS-D03	388 478	936.90	937.59	937.24	0.69
	XS-D3B	436 526	936.83	937.17	937.00	0.34
	XS-D3C	514 608	936.25	936.70	936.47	0.45
	XS-D04	549 654	936.09	936.47	936.28	0.38
Lower Loop D	XS-D05	697 894	934.87	935.37	935.12	0.50
	XS-DDS	776 975	933.69	935.28	934.48	1.59

[a] Cross section distances are based on two separate base ines: one for the combined Upper and Lower Loop D study reach and one for the Loop C study reach Arbitra y upstream origins were used for both base ines Where cross section distances differ by more than 1 0 foot between banks due to channe cu vature both the eft- and right-bank distances espective y a e isted

(2011) estimated at the bathhouse. Holmes and Wagner (2011) computed this estimated velocity using wash lines produced by the 11 June flood on the inside and outside of the Loop C bathhouse. They reasoned that the elevation difference between the two high-water marks (1.25 feet) was equivalent to the velocity head occurring at the outside bathhouse wall. Solving for velocity yields an estimate of 9.0 feet per second for streamflow velocity at this location. The average velocities for the left-overbank subsections of XS-C01 and XS-C1B, the two cross sections which bracket the bathhouse (see fig. 2), are 9.3 and 9.2 feet per second, respectively, using the 40,800-cubic feet per second model.

The difference in computed discharges between the upstream and downstream subreaches for the 40,800-cubic feet per second model (table 7) is among the lowest of all models considered. Based on the slope-area analysis, the discharge difference is 7,900 cubic feet per second for the 40,800-cubic feet per second model. Of the models considered, only one had a smaller difference (7,200 cubic feet per second), but that model produced higher flow velocities in the left-overbank subsection near the bathhouse.

Lastly, the overall discharge of 40,800 cubic feet per second is very close to that independently estimated by Holmes and Wagner (2011) for the 11 June flood using a SAC reach also within the Loop C study reach, but approximately 150 feet upstream of the SAC reach used in this study. Holmes and Wagner (2011) estimated a peak discharge of 40,100 cubic feet per second. They used cross sections in the vicinity of XS-CUS and XS-C01 (fig. 2). The diagnostics for the

Table 4—Manning *n* roughness values determined for cross sections in the Albert Pike Recreation Area study reaches. See text and appendix A for how initial and final roughness values were computed

Study reach	Cross section	Channel[a] station	Initial Manning *n* value			Final Manning *n* value		
			Left overbank	Main channel	Right overbank	Left overbank	Main channel	Right overbank
		feet						
Loop C	XS-CUS	155	0.042	0.057	n/a	0.042	0.061	n/a
	XS-C01	283	0.042	0.057	n/a	0.042	0.061	n/a
	XS-C1B	425	0.045	0.065	n/a	0.045	0.069	n/a
	XS-C02	451	0.045	0.065	n/a	0.045	0.069	n/a
	XS-C03	615	0.043	0.072	n/a	0.043	0.076	n/a
	XS-C3B	742	0.043	0.055	0.036	0.043	0.059	0.036
	XS-C04	828	0.043	0.055	0.036	0.043	0.059	0.036
	XS-C05	926	0.043	0.061	0.035	0.043	0.065	0.035
Upper Loop D	XS-DUS	53	0.087	0.061	n/a	0.085	0.061	n/a
	XS-D01	121	0.066	0.056	n/a	0.064	0.056	n/a
	XS-D1D	135	0.045	0.061	n/a	0.043	0.061	n/a
	XS-D1C	150	0.037	0.064	n/a	0.035	0.064	n/a
	XS-D02	289	0.037	0.066	n/a	0.035	0.066	n/a
	XS-D03	460	0.025	0.064	n/a	0.023	0.064	n/a
	XS-D3B	508	0.026	0.061	n/a	0.024	0.061	n/a
	XS-D3C	589	0.043	0.066	n/a	0.041	0.066	n/a
	XS-D04	633	0.030	0.065	n/a	0.028	0.065	n/a
Lower Loop D	XS-D05	847	0.055	0.069	n/a	0.053	0.069	n/a
	XS-DDS	927	0.060	0.075	n/a	0.058	0.075	n/a

N/A = not applicable
[a] Channel station is the downstream distance where the cross section intersects the longitudinal centerline of the active channel Distance is based on two separate baselines: one for the combined Upper and Lower Loop D study reach and one for the Loop C study reach

Table 5—Comparison of Manning *n* values for Albert Pike Recreation Area study reaches and other locations (Soong and others, no date)

Site	Site description	Maximum flow depth: Roughess height (D_{84})	Slope	Manning *n*
Upper Loop D	DA = 30.4 mi^2; straight channel; D_{84} = 198-479 mm; trees along upper banks	>5.0	0.002-0.006	0.056-0.066
Lower Loop D	DA = 34.0 mi^2; straight channel; D_{84} = 240-375 mm; trees along upper banks	>5.0	0.008-0.010	0.069-0.075
Loop C	Same as Upper Loop D	>5.0	0.004-0.006	0.059-0.076
Merced River at Happy Isles Bridge, near Yosemite, CA	DA = 181 mi^2; straight channel; D_{84} = 550 mm bed material; trees along upper banks	3.33	0.013	0.065
Middle Branch Westfield River at Goss Heights, MA	DA = 52.6 mi^2; straight channel; coarse gravel to boulder bed material; trees along banks	1.14	0.009	0.056
East Branch Ausable River at Au Sable Forks, NY	DA = 198 mi^2; straight channel; gravel to boulder bed material; trees and bushes along banks	3.00	0.006	0.055
Boundary Creek near Porthill, ID	DA = 97 mi^2; straight channel; D_{84} = 375 mm bed material; boulders and trees along banks	4.88	0.019	0.073
Rock Creek Canal near Darby, MT	DA = not listed; straight channel; D_{84} = 375 mm bed material; boulders and bushes along banks	1.63	0.021	0.060

DA = drainage basin area

Holmes and Wagner (2011) model were also quite good. The difference in the discharge estimates between their model and that for the Loop C SAC reach (2 percent) is well below the 10 percent value used by USGS in judging whether two peak discharge estimates differ enough to warrant revising their published records (Novak 1985). Moreover, Holmes estimates of 0.038 and 0.053 for Manning *n* values in the left-overbank and main-channel subsections, respectively[a], are comparable to those associated with the 40,800-cubic feet per second model at XS-CUS and XS-C01 (table 4, Final Manning *n* value columns).

Upper Loop D peak discharge—The 35,600-cubic feet per second model was selected as the best estimate of peak discharge for the 11 June flood in the Upper Loop D study reach. The SAC reach defined by cross sections XS-D1C, XS-D02, and XS-D03 (fig. 3) was used to estimate discharge. The SAC diagnostics for the 35,600-cubic feet per second model (table 7) are generally better than those for all other models considered. The SAC reach in the Upper Loop D study reach does exhibit some expansion between XS-D1C and XS-D02, but spread values are still quite low, *CX* values are close to 1.0, and all *RX* and *RC* values are close to 0. Fall values and conveyance ratios meet the

[a] Holmes, R.R. 2011. Indirect measurement summary Little Missouri River at Albert Pike, Arkansas. 10 p. Administrative report. On file with U.S. Geological Survey, 1400 Independence Road, Rolla, MO 65401.

Table 6—Ratio of flow depth to channel roughness size for cross sections in the Albert Pike Recreation Area study reaches. The bed-material D_{90} is used to represent roughness element size

Study reach	Cross section	Minimum overbank flow depth[a]	Flow depth / D_{90}[b]
		feet	
Loop C	XS-CUS	11.35	5.04
	XS-C01	12.12	5.39
	XS-C1B	12.51	5.56
	XS-C02	12.72	5.65
	XS-C03	13.88	6.17
	XS-C3B	12.03	5.35
	XS-C04	12.15	5.40
	XS-C05	13.66	6.07
Upper Loop D	XS-DUS	16.23	7.21
	XS-D01	15.75	7.00
	XS-D1D	15.78	7.01
	XS-D1C	15.81	7.03
	XS-D02	16.42	7.30
	XS-D03	16.52	7.34
	XS-D3B	15.14	6.73
	XS-D3C	13.00	5.78
	XS-D04	12.40	5.51
Lower Loop D	XS-D05	15.46	6.87
	XS-DDS	14.60	6.49

[a] The minimum overbank flow depth is the difference between the owest e evation at which streamflow wou d spi out of the main-channe banks and onto the adjacent and surface and the tha weg e evation

[b] The D_{90} used for a cross sections is 2 25 feet the maximum observed within a study reaches

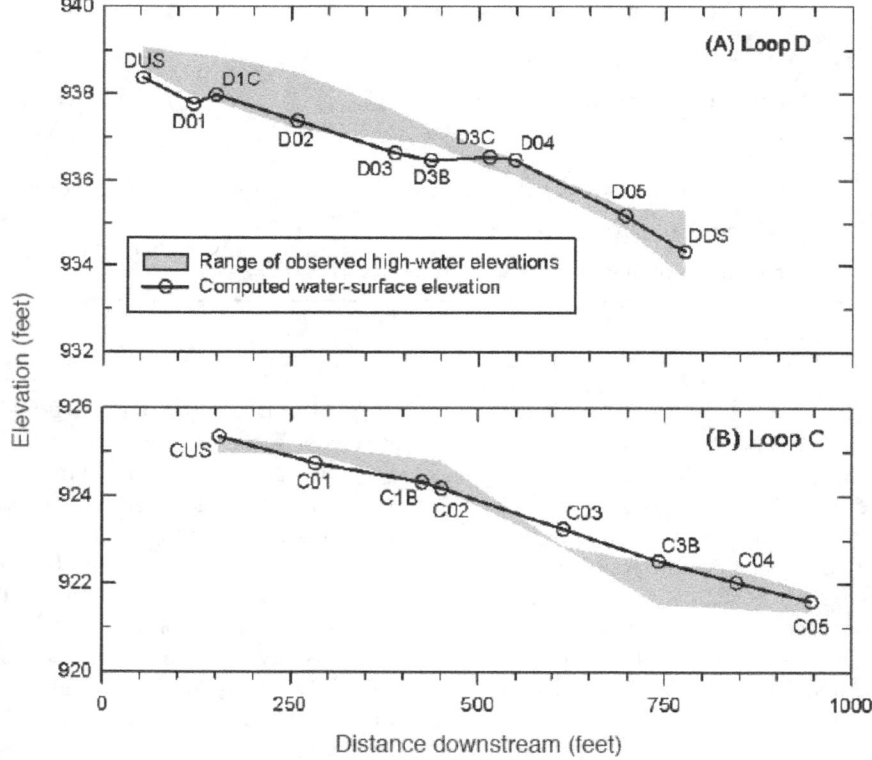

Figure 9   Comparison of observed high-water e evations and computed high-water e evations for the June 11 2010 flood in the combined Loop D (A) and Loop C (B) study reaches Channe cross-section ocations are abe ed using eft-bank base ine distances for each study reach

recommended standards, but just barely. Froude numbers for all subsections and entire cross sections are well below 1.0 (table 7) indicating subcritical flow. Subreach velocity heads are somewhat high relative to fall values, but the ratio of the two for the entire reach is much closer to the recommended value of 1 or less. The friction head for one subreach does exceed the fall value for the one expanding subreach, but not greatly so. Once again, the length-to-depth ratio is well below the recommended value of 75, but this was true of all models considered. Another model actually had as good or slightly better diagnostics than the 35,600-cubic feet per second model except for the conveyance ratio, which was just below the recommended minimum of 0.80 (appendix D). It is for this reason that the 35,600-cubic feet per second model was considered superior.

The computed HWEs using the 35,600-cubic feet per second model generally fit the observed HWEs well (fig. 9A). The computed HWEs for four of the seven cross sections in the Upper Loop D study reach are within the HWE range observed for the respective left and right banks. The three cross sections with computed HWEs outside of their respective ranges, XS D01, D03, and D3B, are 0.37 foot or less than their respective HWE minimums for their left and right banks. None of the other models considered produced HWEs that fit the observed data better than the 35,600-cubic feet per second model, though some fits were just as good. The fit of the computed HWEs in the Lower Loop D study reach was also quite good (fig. 9A). The same changes in roughness values associated with the 35,600-cubic feet per second model were applied to the two cross sections in the Lower Loop D study reach, but HWEs were computed using the 40,800-cubic feet per second discharge estimated for the Loop C study reach. All HWEs for the two cross sections were within the range of observed HWEs for their respective left and right banks.

The 35,600-cubic feet per second model produced the smallest difference in discharges between the two subreaches (table 7). This difference was 100 cubic feet per second.

In comparison to final roughness estimates for Loop C, the final Manning n values associated with the 35,600-cubic feet per second model in the combined Loop D reaches show both similarities and differences where visual evidence suggests that they should. The cross sections in Loop C and the combined Loop D reaches are most similar in their main-channel subsections where substrate sizes (figs. 6 and 7), channel slope, and bank cover conditions are

Table 7—Diagnostics values for slope-area models chosen to compute peak discharge during the June 11, 2010, flood in the Albert Pike Recreation Area study reaches

Study reach	Sub-reach	Fall	Length	Discharge	Spread	CX^a	RC^b	RX^c	Length: Depth > 75	Conveyance ratio	Maximum velocity head:fall	Friction head:fall	Froude number
		------ feet ------		cubic feet per second	percent								
Loop C	C02-C03	1.34	165	45,400	0	1.000	0.133	0	No	1.21	1.18	0.88	0.48-0.53
	C03-C04	1.42	217	37,500	0	1.000	0.202	0	No	0.92	1.32	0.83	0.53-0.62
	All	2.76	382	40,800	0	1.000	0.174	0	No	1.11	0.68	0.85	0.48-0.62
Upper Loop D	D1C-D02	0.5	128	35,600	6	0.968	0	-0.117	No	0.99	2.42	1.06	0.51-0.52
	D02-D03	0.59	156	35,700	0	1.000	0.134	0	No	0.81	2.07	0.88	0.51
	All	1.09	284	35,600	2	0.986	0.066	-0.059	No	0.80	1.12	0.97	0.51-0.52

a The ratio of the computed discharge divided by the discharge computed with no expansion loss (Fulford 1994).
b The ratio of the velocity head change in a contracting reach or subreach divided by the friction head (Fulford 1994).
c The ratio of the velocity head change in the expanding sections of a reach or subreach divided by the friction head (Fulford 1994).

also generally similar. For the main-channel subsections, the estimated roughness values range from 0.056 to 0.077 for cross sections in both the Upper and Lower Loop D study reaches, while those for the Loop C cross sections range from 0.059 to 0.076 (table 4). For the left-overbank subsections, the differences in cover between the two areas are also evident in the roughness values. Loop C has fairly consistent, open forest cover along its left-overbank area, and n values range from 0.042 to 0.045. In contrast, the

combined Loop D reaches have more varied cover with large areas of pavement and short grass between XS-D1C and XS-D04 ($0.023 <= n <= 0.041$), and open to closed forest cover elsewhere ($0.043 <= n <= 0.085$).

Sensitivity analysis—Sensitivity analysis of the discharge final models indicates that varying head drops within the range determined by high-water marks can have a substantial effect on the discharge estimates in both the

(A)

(B)

(C)

(D)

Figure 10   Examp es of different cover types within the study reaches: (A) main-channe ooking upstream from XS-D04 toward XS-D3B and showing both bed materia size distribution and bank cover; (B) ta -grass cover on ups ope side of Forest Service Road 73 in Upper Loop D; (C) pavement and short-grass cover over in Upper Loop D ooking from XS-D3B toward XS-D1C where tree ine begins; and (D) c osed forest cover on right bank of Lower Loop D with red flag (indicated by arrow) at the high-water mark from the June 11 2010 flood

Table 8— Results for selected cases from the sensitivity analysis of slope-area modeling in the Loop C and Upper Loop D study reaches of the Albert Pike Recreation Area. Both discharge and model diagnostic values are listed for each model. See Fulford (1994) for details on computation of diagnostic values

SAC reach	Scenario	Manning n change		Fall	Discharge	Spread	HF[a]	CX[b]	RC[c]	RX[d]	Discharge difference between subreaches	Percent discharge change from selected model
		Left bank	Main channel	feet	cubic feet per second	percent					cubic feet per second	percent
Upper Loop D	Maximum discharge from maximum fall with n change	+0.002	-0.004	1.98	46,700	0	1.739	1	0.139	0	5,000	31.2
	Minimum discharge from maximum fall with n change	-0.004	+0.004	1.98	41,600	0	1.348	1	0.469	0	11,500	16.9
	Discharge from maximum fall with no change	+0.000	+0.000	1.98	44,300	0	1.612	1	0.228	0	7,000	24.4
	Selected model	+0.000	+0.000	1.09	35,600	2	1.052	0.986	0.066	-0.059	100	0.0
	Maximum discharge from n change only	+0.000	-0.004	1.09	38,000	3	1.103	0.982	0.024	-0.072	1,000	6.7
	Minimum discharge from n change only	-0.004	+0.004	1.09	33,200	1	0.867	0.992	0.278	-0.04	4,000	-6.7
Loop C	Maximum discharge from maximum fall with n change	-0.004	-0.004	3.36	47,100	0	2.638	1	0.274	0	15,100	15.4
	Minimum discharge from maximum fall with n change	+0.004	+0.004	3.36	42,100	0	2.783	1	0.207	0	15,200	3.2
	Discharge from maximum fall only	+0.000	+0.000	3.36	44,400	0	2.716	1	0.237	0	15,300	8.8
	Selected model	+0.000	+0.000	2.76	40,800	0	2.35	1	0.174	0	7,900	0.0
	Maximum discharge from minimum fall with n change	-0.004	-0.004	1.86	39,400	1	1.753	0.991	0.079	-0.036	18,600	-3.4
	Minimum discharge from minimum fall with n change	+0.004	+0.004	1.86	34,700	0	1.795	0.996	0.044	-0.017	18,000	-15.0
	Discharge from minimum fall with no change	+0.000	+0.000	1.86	36,900	1	1.777	0.994	0.059	-0.024	18,500	-9.6
	Maximum discharge from n change only	-0.004	+0.004	2.76	43,300	0	2.296	1	0.202	0	7,600	6.1
	Minimum discharge from n change only	+0.004	+0.004	2.76	38,500	0	2.397	1	0.152	0	7,800	-5.6

[a] The total friction head to multiple subsearches (Fulford 1994).
[b] The ratio of the computed discharge divided by the discharge computed with no expansion loss (Fulford 1994).
[c] The ratio of the velocity head change in a contracting reach or subreach divided by the friction head (Fulford 1994).
[d] The ratio of the velocity head change in the expanding sections of a reach or subreach divided by the friction head (Fulford 1994).

Table 9—Regional regression (U.S. Geological Survey 1998) model values and peak-discharge predictions for selected return-period events in Albert Pike Recreation study reaches. The June 11, 2010, flood (computed using the slope-area method) is also listed

Study reach	Drainage area	Mean basin elevation	Basin shape factor	Regression method	Peak discharge[a]				
	mi²	feet			cubic feet per second				
					10-year	25-year	50-year	100-year	June 11, 2010
Loop C and Lower Loop D	33.98	1437	0.24	Unweighted	16,500 (8,690-31,400)	22,400 (11,800-42,700)	27,000 (14,000-51,800)	31,700 (16,200-61,900)	40,800
Loop C				Weighted	17,200	21,100	24,300	27,300	N/A
Upper Loop D	30.38	1444	0.21	Unweighted	14,600 (7,700-27,600)	19,800 (10,400-37,400)	23,700 (12,400-45,400)	27,900 (14,300-54,100)	35,600

N/A = not applicable.

[a] Upper and lower 90-percent prediction limits are listed in parentheses.

Loop C and Upper Loop D SAC reaches. Table 8 lists selected cases from the sensitivity analysis for both SAC reaches to show the range of discharges. Based on the estimated HWEs for the left and right banks of the cross sections, the maximum fall possible in the Loop D SAC reach is 1.98 feet or a 0.89-foot increase from that used in the selected slope-area model. This is the total fall, i.e., the elevation difference between the upstream-most and downstream-most cross sections. Using this fall and varying n values by ±0.004 units from the n values of the selected models, discharge varies from 41,600 to 46,700 cubic feet per second, an increase of 16.9 to 31.2 percent from the discharge for the selected model. For the same fall change scenario with the Loop C SAC reach, the maximum fall is 3.36 feet (a 0.60 foot increase), and discharge range is 42,100 to 47,100, or a 3.2 to 15.4 percent increase. The higher percent change for the Loop D discharges is due in part to the much higher change in fall used there.

A minimum-fall-with-varying-n scenario is only examined for the Loop C SAC reach because this scenario in the Upper Loop D SAC reach results in only 0.2 foot of total fall and models that violate several of the guidelines for reliable slope-area modeling. The minimum-fall scenario for the Loop C SAC reach is 1.86 feet or a 0.9 foot decrease from the selected model. Predicted discharges vary from 34,700 to 39,400 cubic feet per second, and percent changes (-15.0 to -3.4 percent change, respectively) are similar in absolute magnitude to those for the maximum-head-with-varying-n scenario. The minimum-head-with-no-n-change scenario produces a discharge of 36,900 cubic feet per second (-9.6 percent change). When just the n values are varied, discharge ranges between 33,200 and 38,000 cubic feet per second for the Upper Loop D SAC reach, or within ±6.7 percent of the selected model discharge. The same scenario in the Loop C SAC reach produces discharges of 38,500 to 43,300 cubic feet per second, or a -5.6 to 6.1 percent change. These large differences in predicted discharge using HWEs based on observed high-water marks and plausible variations in Manning n values clearly demonstrate the importance of obtaining accurate high-water marks in numerous places and making careful estimates of n values. Furthermore, they also demonstrate the great value in having additional, independent estimates of discharge or other hydraulic values [e.g., Holmes and Wagner (2011)] to help judge the accuracy of slope-area modeling results.

10-, 25-, 50-, and 100-Year Flood Elevations

Flood discharges—The peak discharge predictions for the 10-, 25-, 50-, and 100-year flood events at the APRA study reaches are listed in table 9 along with those for the

11 June flood. As noted previously, the same discharges are used for both Loop C and Lower Loop D study reaches because they are close together (≈ 1500 feet) and there are no significant tributary streams than join the LMR between the two study reaches.

The mean basin elevations for both the Upper Loop D and Loop C study reaches (table 9) are greater than the stated maximum elevation for which the regional-regression models are applicable. The maximum mean basin elevation used to derive the models is 1,250 feet above mean sea level (U.S. Geological Survey 1998) whereas the elevations for Loop C and Upper Loop D are 1,437 and 1,444 feet above mean sea level, respectively (table 9). While the differences are not great (13.9 and 14.4 percent , respectively), this does mean that the models are being applied outside of the data range from which they were derived and that the accuracy of the regression predictions (e.g., the 90-percent prediction interval) cannot be quantified with certainty. Nonetheless, the computed prediction intervals (table 9) do provide a rough measure of accuracy for the peak-discharge estimates.

Using the weighted-regression method generally produces lower peak discharges than the unweighted method at Loop C, especially as the return period increases (table 9). Weighted peak discharges were only computed for the Loop C study reach because it came closest to meeting the minimum basin area criterion for using this method. The percent change between the unweighted and weighted discharge predictions increases with the return period and is almost 14 percent for the 100-year event. However, using the weighted peak discharges does not change the general

Table 10—Hydraulic characteristics during peak discharge for the June 11, 2010, flood in the Albert Pike Recreation Area study reaches

Study reach	Cross section	Energy gradient	Water-surface elevation	Top Width	Maximum flow depth	LOB hydraulic depth	ROB hydraulic depth	Mean flow velocity LOB	MC	ROB
			--------------------------------feet --------------------------------					--- feet/second ---		
Upper Loop D	XS-DUS	0.0057	938.4	465.5	21.6	5.0	—	3.8	11.0	—
	XS-D01	0.0055	937.8	462.5	20.5	4.6	—	4.7	11.9	—
	XS-D1D	0.0049	938.0	462.1	20.8	4.7	—	6.8	10.4	—
	XS-D1C	0.0048	938.0	459.9	20.9	4.6	—	8.2	9.7	—
	XS-D02	0.0049	937.4	464.2	21.9	4.8	—	8.5	9.4	—
	XS-D03	0.0034	936.6	475.6	21.8	4.9	—	10.9	8.0	—
	XS-D3B	0.0034	936.5	470.0	21.3	5.1	—	10.8	8.1	—
	XS-D3C	0.0044	936.5	477.4	20.5	5.7	—	7.7	8.4	—
	XS-D04	0.0022	936.5	507.2	19.8	6.2	—	8.4	6.3	—
Lower Loop D	XS-D05	0.0076	935.2	409.7	23.1	6.1	—	8.1	10.8	—
	XS-DDS	0.0096	934.3	394.7	22.3	6.0	—	8.2	11.4	—
Loop C	XS-CUS	0.0046	925.3	298.3	23.7	8.0	—	9.6	11.0	—
	XS-C01	0.0046	924.7	303.0	24.3	7.6	—	9.3	11.3	—
	XS-C1B	0.0045	924.3	323.7	24.8	8.5	—	9.2	9.9	—
	XS-C02	0.0048	924.2	332.4	23.8	8.0	—	9.1	10.0	—
	XS-C03	0.0062	923.3	367.4	23.1	8.0	—	10.8	9.1	—
	XS-C3B	0.0042	922.5	411.2	22.7	7.8	2.0	8.7	10.6	4.2
	XS-C04	0.0049	922.0	426.9	21.3	7.3	2.3	9.1	10.8	5.1
	XS-C05	0.0058	921.6	464.7	21.4	6.5	2.7	9.1	10.2	6.3

— = not app icab e
LOB = eft-overbank subsection
MC = main-channe subsection
ROB = right-overbank subsection

conclusions about how campground elevations compare to HWEs for 10-, 25-, 50-, and 100-year flood events that are given below. Based on this result, plus the uncertainty in applying the weighted-regression method outside the minimum basin area limit, the weighted discharge predictions were not used.

The standard step analyses for all study reaches shows that the computed HWEs for all flood events are well above the critical-depth elevation for each respective flow, indicating that the assumption of subcritical flow is well supported.

Loop C flood elevations—In the Loop C study reach, the standard step analysis indicates that at the peak of the 11 June flood, maximum flow depths ranged from 21 to 25 feet, and flow widths from 300 to 465 feet (table 10). Mean flow depths (as represented by the hydraulic depth) in the left-overbank area where the Loop C Campground is located were 6.5-8.5 feet, and mean flow velocities were 8.7-10.8 feet per second. The right-overbank area (XS-D03 to XS-D05) where the Loop B Campground is located had mean flow depths of 2.0-2.7 feet, and mean flow velocities of 4.2-6.3 feet per second. The computed HWEs are shown in figure 11 for the 11 June flood at selected cross sections in the Loop C study reach.

Analysis of the other flood events shows that the Loop C Campground is consistently below the 10-year flood elevation, while the Loop B Campground appears to lie near the 25-year flood elevation. Figure 12 shows the computed HWEs for the 10-, 25-, and 100-year events at selected cross sections in the Loop C study reach; table 11 lists the HWEs for all cross sections and events. For the 10-year flood, mean flow depths range from 2.1 to 3.6 feet in the left-overbank area. The right-overbank area only becomes flooded at discharges exceeding the 25-year event. For the 100-year flood, mean flows depths are 5.3-7.1 feet throughout the Loop C Campground, and 1.0-1.5 feet in the Loop B Campground. The spatial extent of predicted flooding in the Loop C study reach is shown in figure 13 for the 10-year flood and in figure 14 for the 100-year flood.

Loop D flood elevations—In the Upper and Lower Loop D study reaches, the maximum flow depths at the peak of the 11 June flood ranged from 20 to 23 feet, and flow widths from 395 to 507 feet (table 10). The computed HWEs are shown in figure 15 for the 11 June flood at selected cross sections in the combined Loop D study reaches. Mean flow depths in the left-overbank (Loop D Campground) area were 4.6-6.2 feet, and mean flow velocities were 3.8-10.9 feet

per second. The range of mean flow velocities in the left-overbank area is greater than that in the Loop C study reach because of the greater differences in cover types throughout this area. The left-overbank subsections for XS-DUS and XS-D01 are the least affected by campground developments. Large portions of both subsections have closed forest cover with greater roughness and thus lower mean flow velocities (3.8-4.7 feet per second). The other cross sections have left-overbank subsections that are much more affected by campground developments, have more open cover types, and experienced much higher flow velocities (6.8-10.9 feet per second).

Analysis of the other flood events shows that almost all of the Loop D Campground area is at or below the 10-year flood elevation. The computed HWEs for the 10-, 25-, and 100-year flood events are shown in figure 16 for selected cross sections in the combined Loop D study reaches, and listed for all events and cross sections in table 11. At XS-D01, essentially the upstream (north) end of the Loop D Campground, the 10-year flood elevation extends from the channel to about 60 feet of FS Rd 73 (fig. 17). This distance decreases to about 35 feet at XS-D03, but floods all of the parking lots and other developments between this location and the main channel. By XS-D04 and continuing downstream, FS Rd 73 and all Loop D Campground developments are now flooded by the 10-year event. For the 25-year event, the only portion of the Loop D Campground that is not flooded is the portion of FS Rd 73 just north of (upstream from) XS-D02 (fig. 16). For the 100-year event, the Loop D Campground lies on average 3.4-4.9 feet below the computed HWE. Figures 17 and 18 show the extent of flooding for the 10- and 100-year events in the combined Loop D study reaches.

Confidence in Results

In judging how much confidence can be placed in the HWEs determined by this investigation, several factors should be considered. The first is how well the methods employed are accepted by the technical community. As noted in the Methods section, the slope-area method, USGS regional-regression models, and the standard step method have all been used extensively and are widely recognized as standard methods for the applications utilized in this study.

The second consideration is how well the assumptions and guidelines for applying these methods are met in a particular application. Many of the features occurring in the SAC reaches permit accurate discharge modeling using the

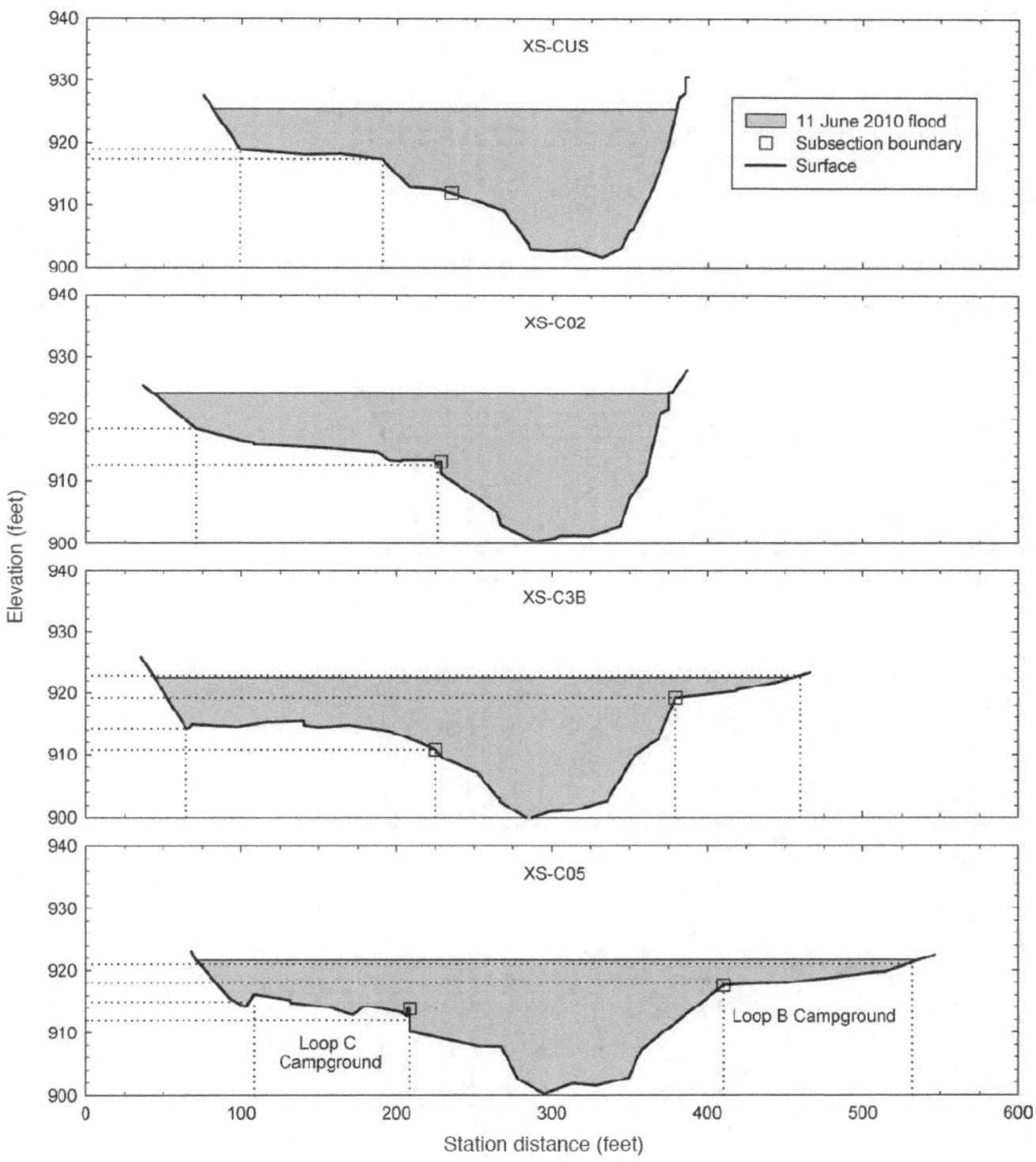

Figure 11   High-water e evations at the 40 800-cubic feet per second peak discharge during the June 11 2010 flood at se ected cross sections in the Loop C study reach View is ooking downstream Dotted ines indicate the vertica and horizonta positions of the Loops B and C campgrounds within each cross section

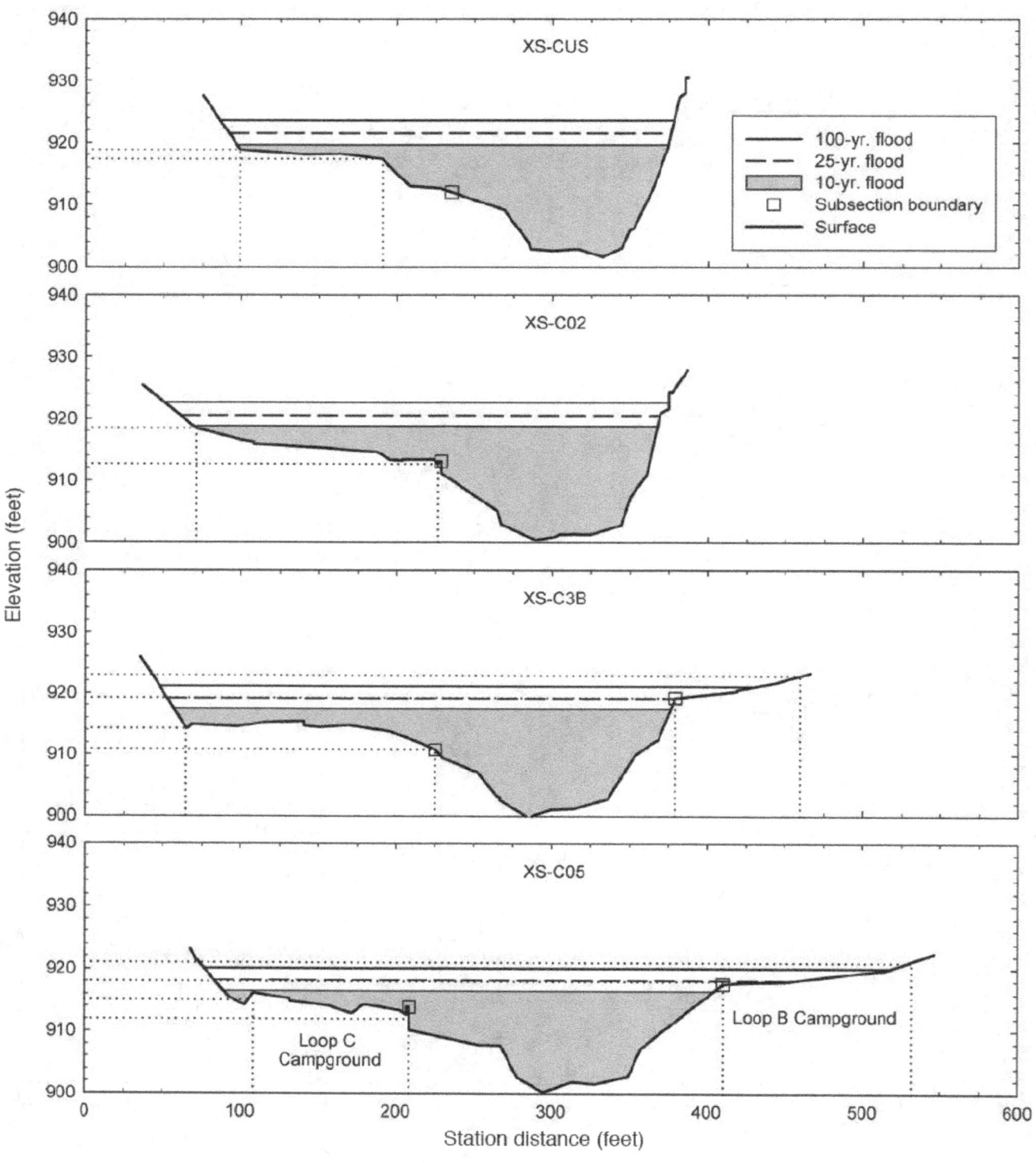

Figure 12 Computed high-water e evations for the 10- 25- and 100-year flood events at se ected cross sections in the Loop C study reach Dotted ines indicate the vertica and horizonta positions of the Loops B and C campgrounds within each cross section

slope-area method. Channel orientation is generally straight within the SAC reaches, with flow paths either contracting or exhibiting only minor expansion. Cross-sectional shape is generally uniform throughout the SAC reaches, with no abrupt changes in geometry or significant flow obstructions occurring. There is no evidence that significant ponding, scour, or fill occurred in the SAC reaches during the 11 June flood.

Of the numerous guidelines for accurately employing the slope-area method, only three were unmet by the conditions present in the two SAC reaches:

- The velocity heads were somewhat greater than the fall values in both SAC reaches (table 7).
- Reach length-to-depth ratios were well below 75.
- The friction head-to-fall ratio was greater than 1.0 for one subreach (D1C-D02).

In addition, the minimum fall and conveyance ratio criteria were just barely met for two subreaches (table 7). These factors do not invalidate use of the slope-area method, but they do suggest that the discharge predictions are less accurate than ideal conditions would permit. Model diagnostics indicate that the quality of the discharge predictions is good for both Loop C and Upper Loop D SAC reaches. However, the sensitivity analysis shows that discharge predictions could vary by approximately ±10 and +25 percent in Loop C and Upper Loop D study reaches, respectively, depending on which HWEs are used to compute fall values. There are no definitive rules for assessing how much these factors affect the accuracy of the discharge prediction; rather professional judgment has be used to weigh these factors against all the others. Taking all factors into account, I think the accuracy of the discharge predictions should be rated as fair.

Table 11—Computed high-water elevations for the 10-, 25-, 50-, and 100-year flood events at cross sections in the Albert Pike Recreation Area study reaches

Study reach	Cross section	High-water elevation			
		10-year	25-year	50-year	100-year
		--------------------feet--------------------			
Upper Loop D	XS-DUS	934.1	935.4	936.3	937.1
	XS-D01	933.7	935.0	935.8	936.5
	XS-D1D	933.7	935.0	935.8	936.6
	XS-D1C	933.6	935.0	935.8	936.6
	XS-D02	933.1	934.4	935.2	936.0
	XS-D03	932.4	933.7	934.5	935.3
	XS-D3B	932.1	933.4	934.3	935.1
	XS-D3C	932.0	933.4	934.3	935.1
	XS-D04	932.0	933.3	934.2	935.1
Lower Loop D	XS-D05	930.1	931.6	932.6	933.6
	XS-DDS	929.3	930.8	931.8	932.7
Loop C	XS-CUS	919.7	921.5	922.6	923.6
	XS-C01	919.2	921.0	922.1	923.1
	XS-C1B	918.9	920.6	921.7	922.7
	XS-C02	918.8	920.5	921.6	922.6
	XS-C03	918.1	919.8	920.9	921.8
	XS-C3B	917.5	919.1	920.2	921.1
	XS-C04	917.0	918.7	919.7	920.6
	XS-C05	916.5	918.2	919.2	920.1

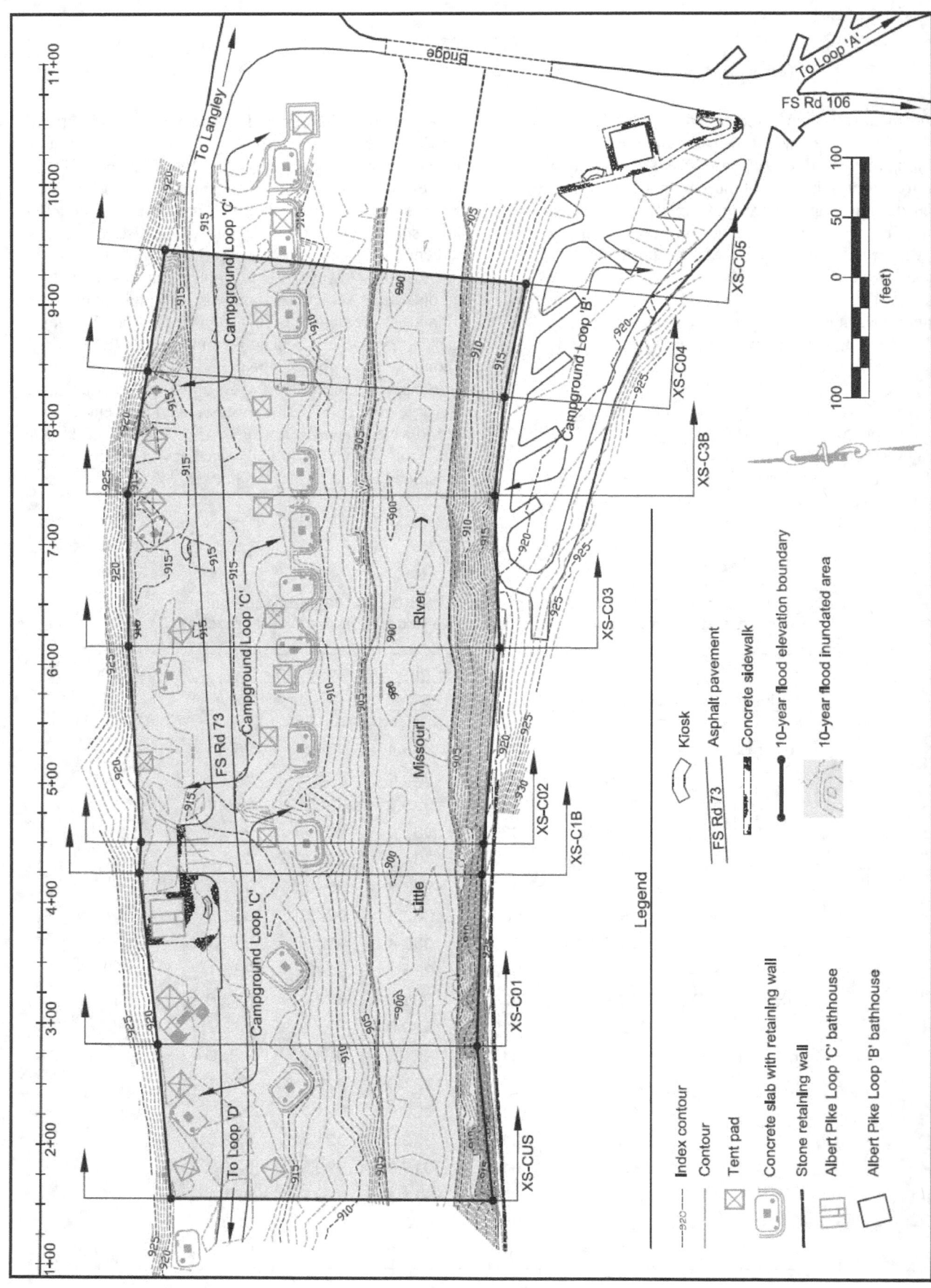

Figure 13—Extent of 10-year flood in the Loop C study reach.

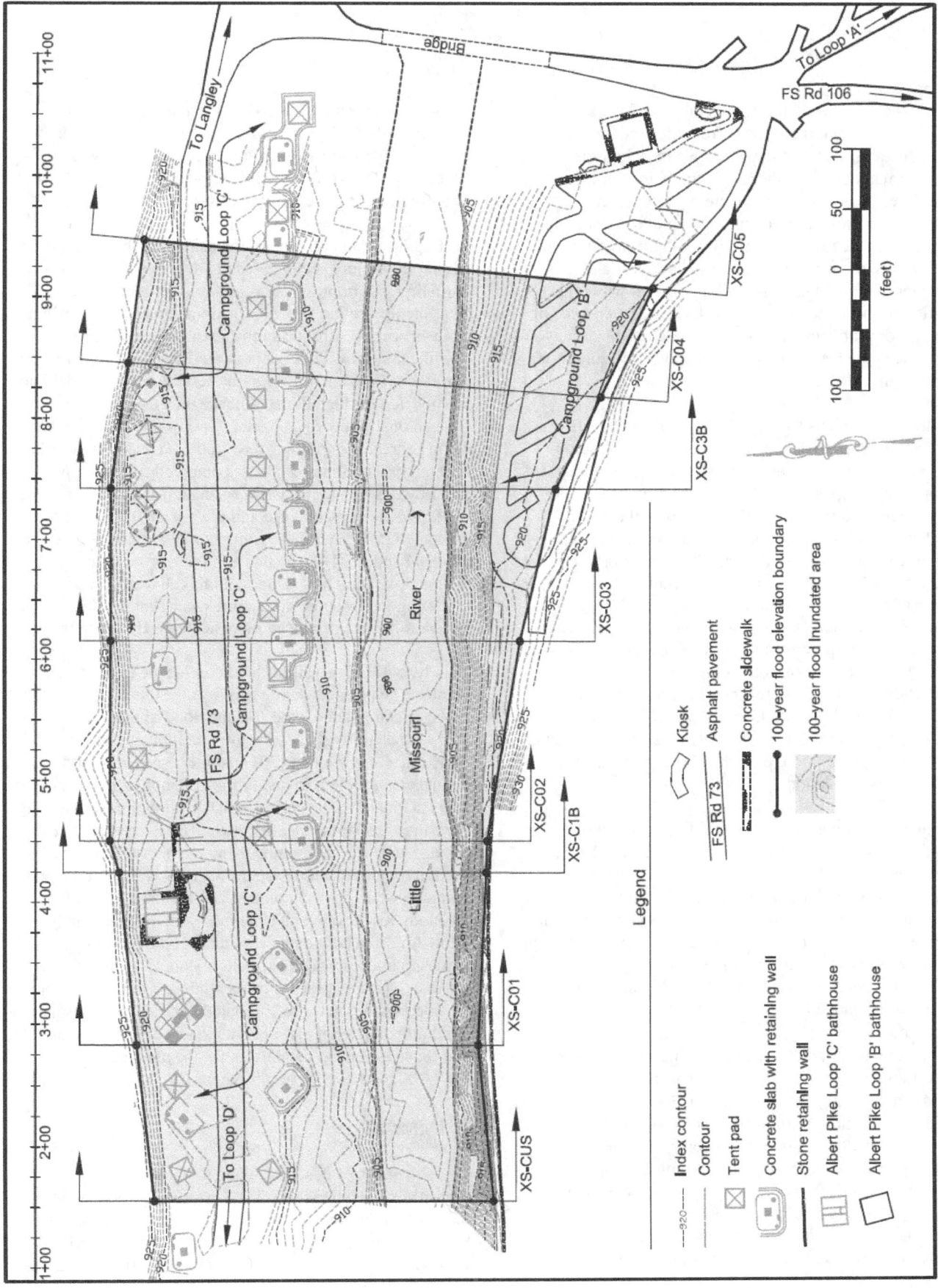

Figure 14—Extent of 100-year flood in the Loop C study reach.

It is likely that the shortcomings in using the slope-area method noted above largely result from the fact that mountain streams such as the LMR have morphologies that vary a great deal over short longitudinal distances. Changes in channel geometry, gradient, bank cover, and bed material composition are frequent along mountain streams as they are influenced by underlying geologic structure, vegetation dynamics, water and sediment inputs, and human interventions. This reality suggests that while this application of the slope-area method failed to meet some of the criteria for producing the most accurate results, it may have produced the best results possible given the conditions that exist in the APRA.

One of the assumptions for applying the regional-regression equations to predict peak discharges for the APRA study reaches was not met. Because the mean basin elevations for the Loop C and Upper Loop D drainage basins are outside the data range used to develop the equations, the accuracy the predicted discharges in table 9 is uncertain. However, the predicted discharges are the best that can be produced given the available methods. The 90-percent prediction intervals (table 9) show that the true discharge for a given flood may lie within a relatively wide range. It is standard practice in flood mapping studies to use the discharge values predicted by the regression equations (National Research Council 2009), as was done for this study. However, one could use a higher discharge from the upper portion of a given prediction interval to compute HWEs and gain greater certainty that a given flood (e.g., the 100-year event) would not exceed these elevations.

All applications of the standard step analysis met the assumptions and guidelines for using this method. The channel orientation, shape uniformity, and lack of flow impediment characteristics noted above for the SAC reaches are also true for the larger study reaches and have a similar advantageous effect on the standard step modeling accuracy. For all flows considered, the assumption of subcritical flow was met at all cross sections. In the Loop C study reach, Froude numbers ranged from 0.33 to 0.48 at all cross sections, and computed critical depths were 3.5 to 7.2 feet below the flood HWEs; in the Upper and Lower Loop D study reaches, Froude numbers were 0.28 to 0.52 and critical depths 2.3 to 6.2 feet below. Energy slopes between cross sections varied from 0.0032 to 0.0063 in Loop C and 0.0022 to 0.0096 in the combined Loop D study reaches, and were well below the 0.10 limit for applying the energy equation (Brunner 2010b). Cross sections and topography within the study reaches were all derived from the same data source; therefore potential errors from using different data sources (Tate and others 2002) are avoided.

At one cross section, XS-DDS, the slice/secant method (Brunner 2010b) had to be used to solve for critical depth; in all other cases the standard parabolic method was successful. This difference in computation method should not affect the accuracy of the results.

Testing has shown that two-dimensional hydraulic modeling can produce more accurate results than one-dimensional modeling, but improvements are most notable when multiple flowpaths, flow obstructions, or significant tributary inflows occur (Transportation Research Board 2006). Significant inflow does occur at the Brier Creek confluence, and it was found that HWEs for the 11 June flood could not be modeled through the confluence area using the one-dimensional standard step analysis. For this reason, the Loop D area was split into two study reaches and modeled separately. The June 11 HWEs computed for the Upper and Lower Loop D study reaches matched up quite well at the Brier Creek confluence and fell within 0.2 feet of the estimated HWE and well within the HWE range observed at XS-D04 and XS-D05, so this approach proved satisfactory. Using a two-dimensional model might have permitted modeling the Loop D area as one reach, but would not necessarily have produced more accurate HWEs in this case.

Finally, other observations lend confidence to the study results. The peak discharge and average left-overbank flow velocity computed for the 11 June flood in the Loop C study reach are very close to those computed independently by Holmes and Wagner (2011) at the same location. Flow depths are sufficient to justify the assumption that roughness is constant above the elevation where streamflow overspills the banks and somewhat below the HWE for the 10-year flood. The HWEs computed using the discharges and cross-section roughness values determined for the 11 June flood compare well with the range of HWEs observed throughout the study reaches. Results from the 11 June flood analysis allow for more confident estimation of the Manning n values than does visual estimation alone. Furthermore, the n values estimated for the cross sections seem reasonable when compared to those computed at other locations having similar bed material and main-channel cover types (table 5), and those estimated by Holmes for the area including XS-CUS and XS-C01 (see footnote 1).

SUMMARY

The objectives of this study were to determine the high-water elevations (HWEs) for selected flood events in the Albert Pike Recreation Area (APRA) and assess how these elevations compare to those for the existing APRA campgrounds. An analysis of the 11 June 2010 flood at the

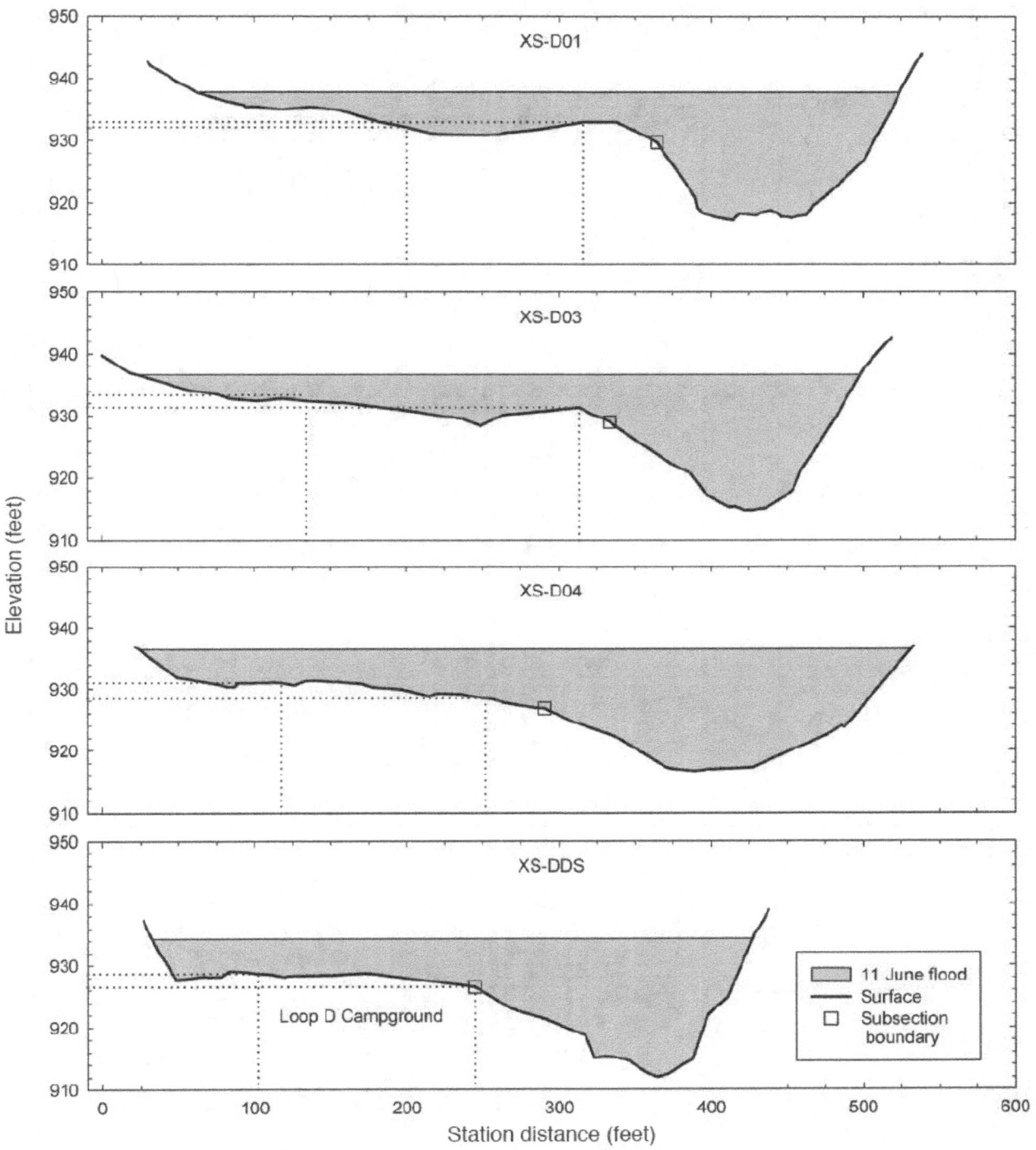

Figure 15 High-water e evations at the 35 600- and 40 800-cubic feet per second peak discharges during the June 11 2010 flood at se ected cross sections of the Upper and Lower Loop D study reaches respective y View is ooking downstream Dotted ines indicate the vertica and horizonta positions of the Loop D campground within each cross section

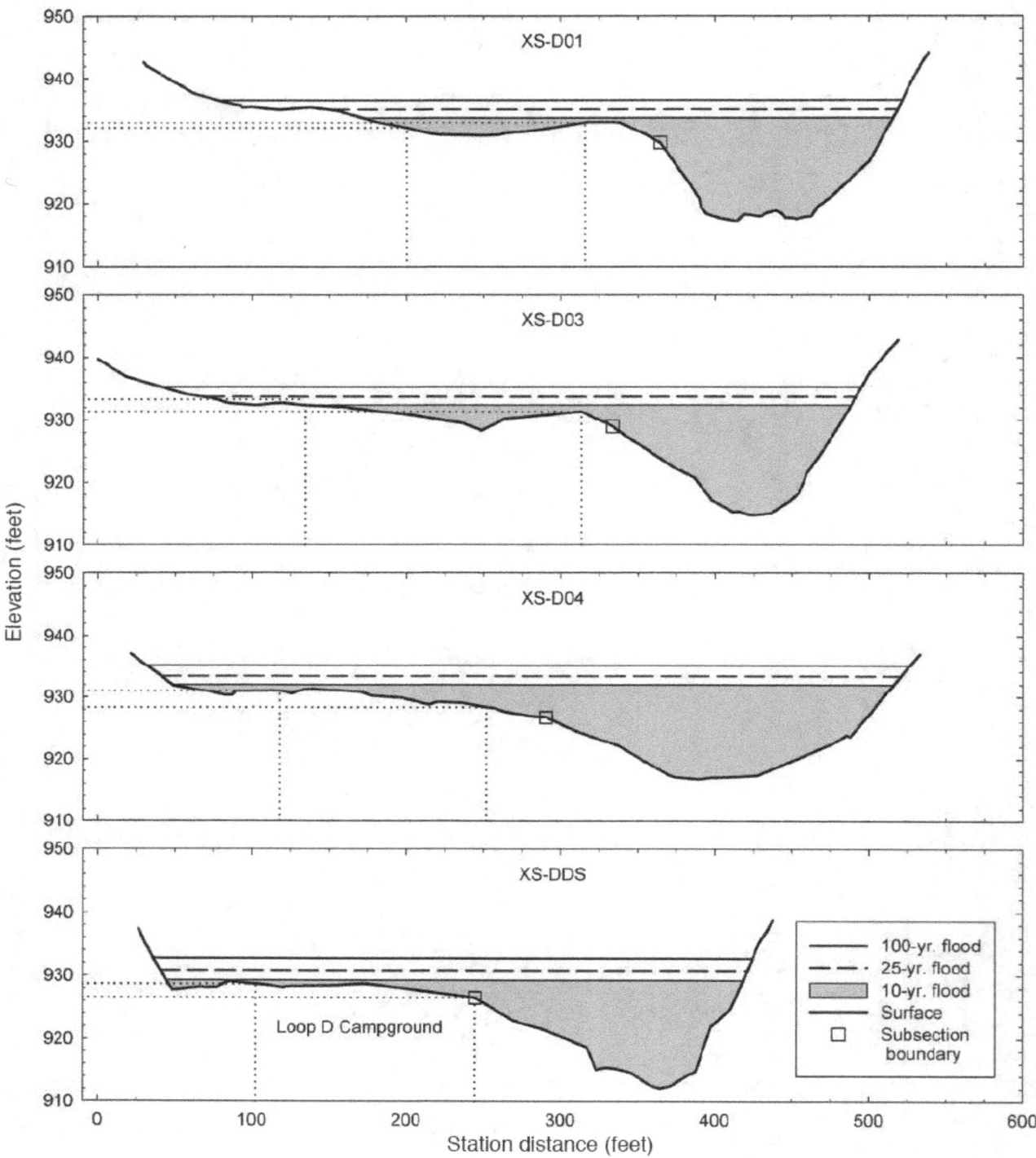

Figure 16   Computed high-water e evations for the 10- 25- and 100-year flood events at se ected cross sections in the A bert Pike Recreation Area Upper and Lower Loop D study reaches Dotted ines indicate the vertica and horizonta positions of the Loop D campground within each cross section

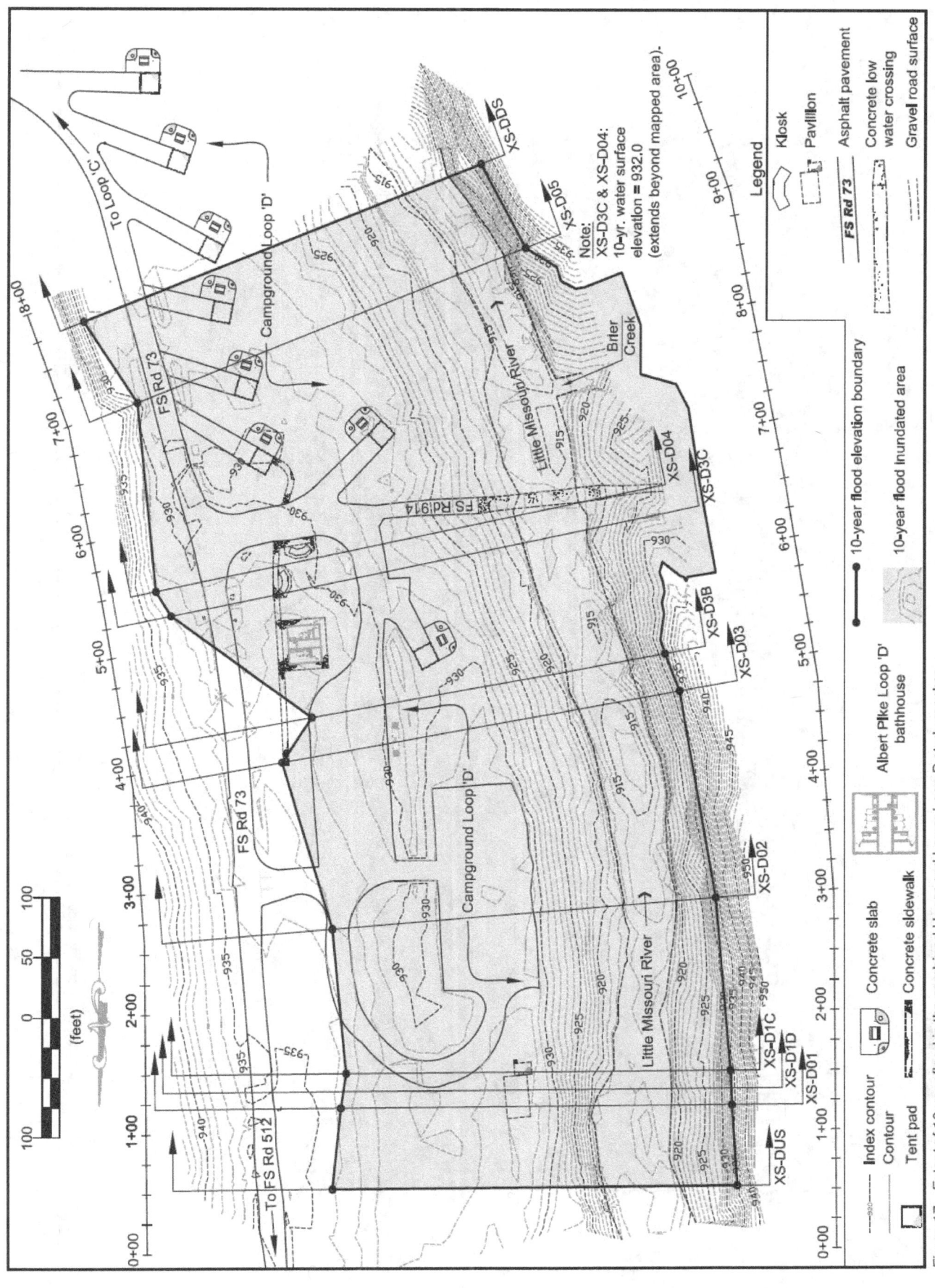

Figure 17.—Extent of 10-year flood in the combined Upper and Lower Loop D study reaches.

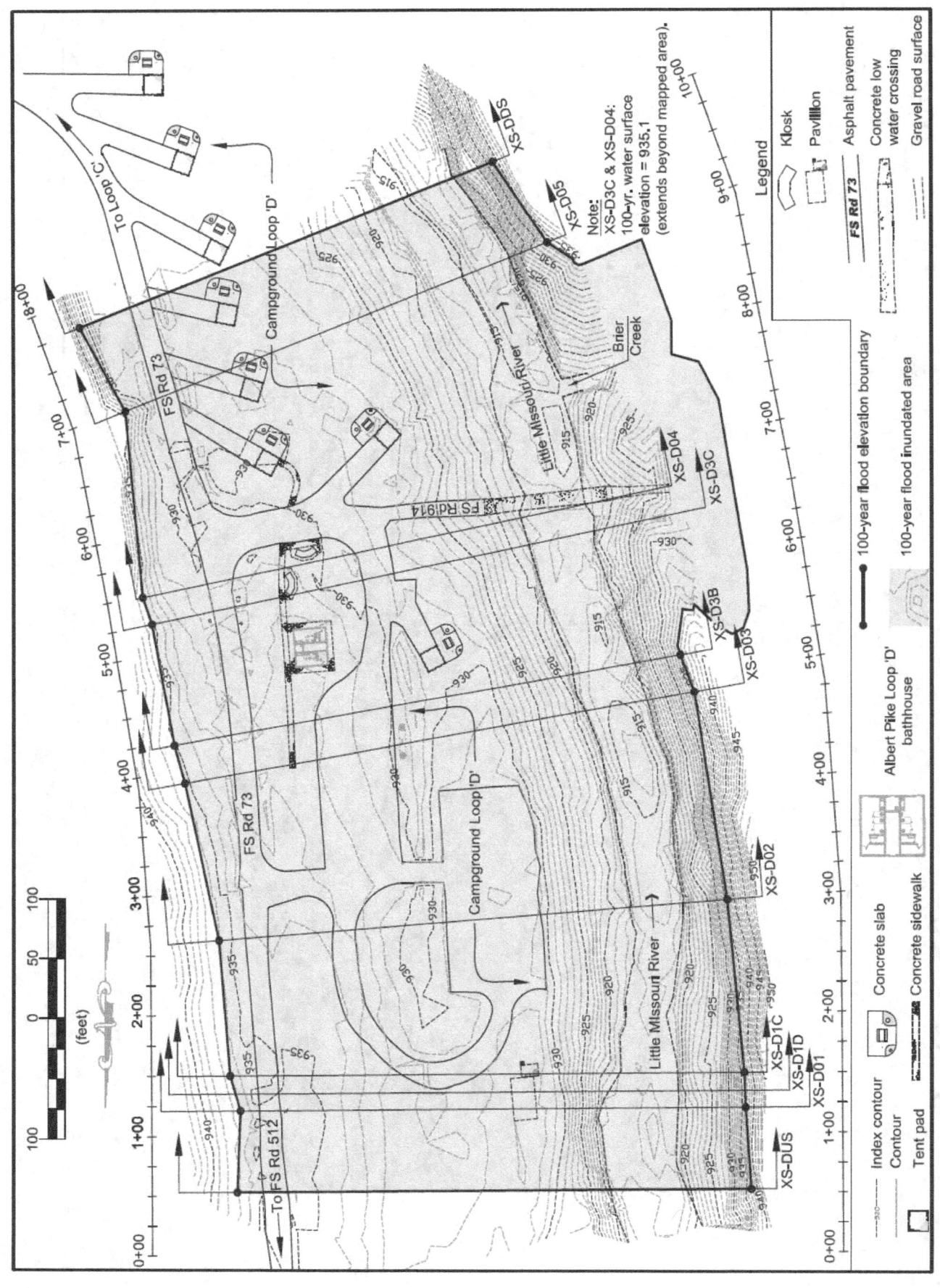

Figure 18—Extent of 100-year flood in the combined Upper and Lower Loop D study reaches.

APRA allows the hydraulic characteristics of this event to be determined and then used to estimate HWEs for the 10-, 25-, 50-, and 100-year flood events in the Loop B, C, and D Campgrounds. The APRA was divided into three study reaches: (1) Loop C, (2) Upper Loop D, and (3) Lower Loop D (fig. 1). Using slope-area modeling and model diagnostics, a group of 3-4 candidate discharge models for the 11 June flood were identified for the Loop C and Upper Loop D Slope Area Computation (SAC) reaches (figs. 2 and 3). Standard step analysis was used to determine how well the computed HWEs determined using the discharge and roughness values for each candidate model matched observed HWEs throughout the three study reaches. For the Lower Loop D study reach, the HWE modeling used discharge values from the Loop C SAC reach and roughness values based on the Upper Loop D SAC reach. The best discharge models for the three study reaches were selected based on model diagnostic values and model fits to observed HWEs. Results indicate that peak discharge during the 11 June flood was 40,800 cubic feet per second in the Loop C and Lower Loop D study reaches, and 35,600 cubic feet per second in the Upper Loop D study reach. This analysis also provides estimates of the roughness values in the study reaches (table 4) which are then used in modeling HWEs for the 10-, 25-, 50-, and 100-year floods.

Standard step modeling of HWEs for the 10-, 25-, 50-, and 100-year floods shows that the Loop C and D Campgrounds are located at or below the 10-year flood elevation (figs. 12, 13, 16, and 17), while the Loop B Campground is located close to the 25-year flood elevation (fig. 12). Peak discharges for the selected flood events were computed using regional-regression equations (Hodge and Tasker 1995, U.S. Geological Survey 1998). With respect to the 100-year flood, the mean flow depths modeled at study reach cross sections indicate that the elevations of the Loop B, C, and D Campgrounds are on average 1.0-1.5, 5.3-7.1, and 3.4-4.9 feet below the computed 100-year HWE, respectively. At its peak, the 11 June flood produced mean flow depths of 2.0-2.7, 6.5-8.5, and 4.6-6.2 feet, respectively, in the Loop B, C, and D Campgrounds (table 10) (figs. 11 and 15).

The methods used for this study—slope-area, regional-regression, and standard step—are widely accepted and used in similar flood modeling and flood mapping assessments (National Research Council 2009, Rantz 1982). The applications of these methods in the present study meet most of the criteria or guidelines specified in the literature or by past practice. Failure to meet all of these guidelines reduces the absolute accuracy of the affected results. However, multiple lines of evidence suggest that the reported results are reasonable and might well be as accurate as the existing conditions at the APRA will allow.

ACKNOWLEDGMENTS

This project would not have occurred without the help of many people. Alan Clingenpeel played a key role in championing the project, assisting with the field work, facilitating my assistance requests to Ouachita National Forest staff, and helping in numerous other ways. Norm Wagoner (Forest Supervisor, Ouachita National Forest) requested that I undertake this project and made Forest resources and personnel available to me. Chad Yocum and Rob Moore deserve special credit for their long hours in the field and extensive AutoCAD efforts (Rob). The efforts of Kim Mortenson, Brady Duff, Stanley Moore, Jonathan Fentress, Tim Brooks, and Syr Johnathan Duncan produced excellent field data. Bob Holmes and Dan Wagner graciously answered all my questions and freely provided their expertise and data. Mark Adams provided both spatial data and his GIS expertise. This report was improved using the insightful reviews provided by Rick Huizinga, Dan Wagoner, Bill Elliot, Alan Clingenpeel, Tony Crump, and Gary Kuhlmann. My thanks to all of these individuals, and all others who helped but are not named here. This project was supported by funding from the U.S. Department of Agriculture Forest Service Southern Research Station and the Ouachita National Forest.

LITERATURE CITED

Arcement, G.J.; Schneider, V.R. 1989. Guide for selecting Manning's roughness coefficients for natural channels and flood plains. U.S. Geological Survey Water Supply Paper 2339. Washington, DC U.S. Geological Survey. 38 p.

Benson, M.A.; Dalrymple, T. 1967. General field and office procedures for indirect discharge measurements. Techniques of water resource investigations of the United State Geological Survey Chapter A1. Washington, DC Government Printing Office. 30 p.

Bevenger, G.S.; King, R.M. 1995. A pebble count procedure for assessing watershed cumulative effects. Res. Pap. RM RP 319. Fort Collins, CO U.S. Department of Agriculture Forest Service, Rocky Mountain Forest and Range Experiment Station. 17 p.

Bray, D.I.; Davar, K.S. 1987. Resistance to flow in gravel-bed rivers. Canadian Journal of Civil Engineering. 14 77-86.

Brunner, G.W. 2010a. HEC RAS River Analysis system user's manual. Davis, CA U.S. Army Corps of Engineers, Hydrologic Engineering Center. 766 p.

Brunner, G.W. 2010b. HEC RAS— River analysis system hydraulic reference manual. Davis, CA U.S. Army Corps of Engineers, Hydrologic Engineering Center. 411 p.

Dalrymple, T.; Benson, M.A. 1968. Measurement of peak discharge by the slope area method. USGS—TWRI Book 3, Chapter A2. Washington, DC U.S. Government Printing Office. 12 p.

Davidian, J. 1984. Computation of water surface profiles in open channels. USGS—TWRI Book 3, Chapter A15. Washington, DC U.S. Government Printing Office. 48 p.

Federal Emergency Management Agency. 2010a. Numerical Models Meeting the Minimum Requirements of the National Flood Insurance Program. http //www.fema.gov/plan/prevent/fhm/en_modl.shtm. [Date accessed June 7, 2001].

Federal Emergency Management Agency. 2010b. Floodplain Modeling Manual HEC-RAS Procedures for HEC-2 Modelers. http //www.fema. gov/plan/prevent/fhm/dl_fpmm.shtm. [Date accessed June 7, 2001].

Fulford, J.M. 1994. User's guide to SAC, a computer program for computing discharge by slope area method. U.S. Geological Survey Open File Report 94 360. Stennis Space Center, MS U.S. Geological Survey. 31 p.

Griffiths, G.A. 1981. Flow Resistance in Coarse Gravel Bed Rivers. Journal of the Hydraulics Division, American Society of Civil Engineers. 107(HY7) 899-918.

Haley, B.R.; Stone, C.G.; geologic mappers; Handson, W.D. ed.; Horvath, S.; Taylor, N. comps. Geologic map of the Big Fork Quadrangle, Montogomery and Polk Counties, Arkansas. 2010. Little Rock, AR Arkansas Geological Survey. 1 24,000; colored. http //www.geology. arkansas.gov/maps_pdf/geologic/24k_maps/Big_Fork.pdf. [Date accessed April 18, 2011]

Herschy, R.W. 1995. Streamflow measurement. 2d ed. London E&FN Spon. 524 p.

Hodge, S.A.; Tasker, G.D. 1995. Magnitude and frequency of floods in Arkansas. U.S. Geological Survey Water Resources Investigations Report 95 4224. 52 p.

Holmes, R.R., Jr.; Wagner, D M. 2011. Flood of June 11, 2010, in the Upper Little Missouri watershed, Arkansas. Scientific Investigations Report 2011-5194. Reston, VA U.S. Geological Survey. 31 p.

Jarrett, R.D. 1987. Evaluation of the slope-area method for computing peak discharge. U.S. Geological Survey Water Supply Paper 2310 13-24.

Kirby, W.H. 1987. Linear error analysis of slope area discharge determinations. In Kirby, W.H.; Hua, S. Q.; Beard, L.R., eds. Analysis of Extraordinary Flood Events. Journal of Hydrology. 96 125 138.

Limerinos, J.T. 1970. Determination of the Manning coefficient from measured bed roughness in natural channels. Water-supply paper 1898-B. Washington, DC U.S. Geological Survey. 47 p.

Mastin, M.C.; Kresch, D.L. 2005. Verification of 1921 peak discharge at Skagit River near Concrete, Washington, using 2003 peak discharge data. U.S. Geological Survey Scientific Investigations Report 2005 5029. 18 p.

Meyer-Peter, E.; Muller, R. 1948. Formulas for bed-load transport. In Proceedings of the International Association for Hydraulic Research, Third Annual Conference. Stockholm, Sweden. [place of publication unknown] [publisher unknown] 39-64.

National Research Council. 2009. Mapping the zone improving flood map accuracy. Committee on FEMA Flood Maps. Washington, DC National Academy Press. 136 p.

Novak, C.E. 1985. WRD data reports preparation guide. U.S. Geological Survey Water Resources Division. 199 p.

Olson, J.W. 2003. Soil survey of Polk county, Arkansas. [Place of publication unknown] U.S. Department of Agriculture, Natural Resources Conservation Service. 391 p.

Olson, J.W. 2007. Soil survey of Montgomery county, Arkansas. [Place of publication unknown] U S. Department of Agriculture, Natural Resources Conservation Service. 613 p.

Rantz, S.E. 1982. Measurement and computation of streamflow Volume 1—Measurement of stage and discharge. U.S. Geological Survey Water Supply Paper 2175. 284 p.

Rosgen, D. 1996. Applied river morphology. Pagosa Springs, CO Wildland Hydrology. [Various pagination].

Shen, H.W.; Julien, P.Y. 1993. Erosion and sediment transport. In Maidment, D.R., ed. Handbook of hydrology. New York McGraw-Hill 12.1–12.61.

Soong, D.T.; Halfar, T.M.; Prater, C.D.; Wobig, L.A. [N.d.]. Estimating Manning's Roughness Coefficients for Natural and Man-Made Streams in Illinois. U.S. Geological Survey. http //il.water.usgs.gov/proj/nvalues/. [Date accessed April 7, 2011].

U.S. Geological Survey. 1998. The National Flood Frequency Program— Methods for Estimating Flood Magnitude and Frequency in Rural Areas in Arkansas. USGS Fact Sheet 128 97. http //pubs.usgs.gov/fs/fs 128 97/ pdf/arkansasfinal.pdf. [Date accessed March 18, 2011].

Van Haveren, B.P. 1986. Water resource measurements a handbook for hydrologists and engineers. Denver, CO American Water Works Association. 132 p.

Wolman, G.M. 1954. A method of sampling coarse river bed material. Transactions, American Geophysical Union. 35(6) 951 956.

Glossary_____

Bankfull—The elevation or discharge at which streamflow fills the channel and just begins to spill out of the channel and onto the adjacent land surface. In alluvial channels, the adjacent land surface is often the floodplain.

Basin shape factor—The upstream drainage area divided by the main channel length for a given location on a stream. Used in Arkansas regional-regression equations to estimate peak discharge magnitude for selected return periods (Hodge and Tasker 1995, U.S. Geological Survey 1998).

Channel geometry—The shape characteristics of a channel cross section based on a lower and upper reference elevation (e.g., the lowest elevation within the cross section and a given water-surface elevation, respectively). It is usually established using a series of distance and elevation measurements along the cross section. From these measurements, a variety of shape metrics such as cross-sectional area, top width, and hydraulic depth can be computed to describe specific shape characteristics.

Conveyance—A measure of the water carrying capacity of a channel at a cross section. Used in the slope-area method to calculate discharge.

Conveyance ratio—The upstream cross section conveyance divided by the downstream cross section conveyance. A diagnostic value for evaluating the accuracy of a slope-area discharge model.

Critical flow—Critical flow occurs when streamflow specific energy (the sum of the flow depth and velocity head and expressed as a depth) is minimum for a given discharge. This flow naturally occurs whenever water passes over a waterfall of similar feature and the streamflow loses contact with the channel surface. **Subcritical flow** occurs whenever streamflow depth is greater than that occurring at critical flow; while **supercritical flow** occurs whenever depth is less than that at critical flow. Where critical flow occurs determines how streamflow hydraulics are modeled.

CX—The ratio of the computed discharge divided by the discharge computed with no expansion loss (Fulford 1994). A diagnostic value for evaluating the accuracy of a slope-area discharge model.

D_x—The grain-size diameter at which x percent of the sampled grains are less than that size. For example, the D_{50} is the diameter size at which 50 percent of the sampled grains are less than that size, and the D_{84} is the size at which 84 percent are less.

Discharge—The volume of water that passes through a channel cross section per unit of time. Streamflow is measured in cubic feet per second in U.S. customary units.

Energy slope or gradient—The difference in total head between an upstream and downstream location divided by the horizontal distance between the two locations. If the flow velocity is the same at both locations, then the energy gradient is equivalent to the water-surface slope.

Entrenchment ratio—As defined by Rosgen (1996), the ratio of the flood-prone area width to the bankfull channel width. The flood-prone area width is the cross-sectional width measured at the elevation equal to twice the bankfull channel maximum depth.

Fall—The difference in water-surface elevation between an upstream and downstream location within a reach or subreach. Fall is the same as head drop.

Friction head—The energy loss, expressed in terms of head, due to frictional forces resisting fluid motion within a conduit or open channel.

Froude number—The ratio of a characteristic velocity to a gravitational wave velocity. In hydraulic situations like streamflow in a natural channel or canal, the mean streamflow velocity (v) is used as the characteristic velocity and the wave velocity is given by the square root of the gravitation acceleration (g) times the mean streamflow depth (d):

$$Fr = \frac{v}{\sqrt{gd}}$$

The Froude number indicates the energy state of streamflow: if $Fr < 1$, then flow is subcritical; if $Fr > 1$, then flow is supercritical; and if $Fr = 1$, then flow is critical.

Head—The energy in a fluid at a given location expressed in terms of a vertical length (i.e., an elevation or height). The total head at a given point in a fluid is determined by the energy associated with the motion of the fluid (the velocity head), the static pressure within the fluid (the pressure head), and the height of the fluid above a given datum (the elevation head).

Head drop—See "Fall."

HF—The total friction head for multiple subreaches (Fulford 1994). A diagnostic value for evaluating the accuracy of a slope-area discharge model.

High-water elevation—The maximum elevation of streamflow above a given datum attained during a given flow event. In most natural streams, this elevation is attained when the maximum discharge occurs for the event.

High-water mark—Physical marks or features that provide evidence of where the **high-water elevation** occurred during a flood.

Hydraulic depth—A measure of streamflow depth equal to the streamflow cross section area divided by the top-width. For most natural channels where streamflow width is much greater than depth, the hydraulic depth is often considered equivalent to the mean streamflow depth.

Mean basin elevation—The average ground elevation, in meters above sea level, measured from topographic maps using a grid sampling method (20 to 80 points sampled in basin) (Hodge and Tasker 1995). Used in computing peak discharge from regional-regression equations developed by the USGS.

Main channel length—The straight-line distance (in km) between the basin divide and a given location on a stream. Used in Arkansas regional-regression equations to estimate peak discharge magnitude for selected return periods (Hodge and Tasker 1995, U.S. Geological Survey 1998).

Normal depth—The flow depth that occurs within an open channel exhibiting uniform streamflow. Uniform streamflow occurs when there is no longitudinal change in flow velocity along the channel. For such flow to occur, the channel must be straight and have a uniform cross section and slope.

RC—The ratio of the velocity head change in a contracting reach or subreach divided by the friction head (Fulford 1994). A diagnostic value for evaluating the accuracy of a slope-area discharge model.

Reach—A general term used to indicate a length of stream channel that has relatively consistent width, depth, slope, and roughness characteristics. A **subreach** is a portion of a reach where these physical characteristics are even more consistent than in the reach as a whole.

Roughness—The characteristic of a channel or ground surface that resists the flow of water. Several metrics over time have been developed to measure roughness, with the Manning *n* value being most often used in the United States.

RX—The ratio of the velocity head change in the expanding sections of a reach or subreach divided by the friction head (Fulford 1994). A diagnostic value used for evaluating the accuracy of a slope-area discharge model.

Siliceous mineralogy—Rocks or sediments containing abundant quartz or other silica minerals.

Spread—The percent difference between discharge computed with no expansion or contraction losses and the discharge computed with full expansion or contraction losses (Fulford 1994). A diagnostic value for evaluating the accuracy of a slope-area discharge model.

Thermic temperature regime—A classification criteria applied to soils wherein the mean annual soil temperature is between 59° and 72° F, and the difference between mean summer and mean winter soil temperature is more than 41° F at a standard reference depth.

Top width—The cross-sectional width of streamflow at the water surface.

Udic moisture regime—A criteria used to classify soils wherein the soil moisture within a standardized location is not dry for more the 90 continuous days in most years.

Velocity head—The energy of a fluid, expressed in terms of head, due to its bulk motion. It is a component of the total head occurring at a given location in a flow conduit or open channel.

Water year—A continuous 12-month period defined to encompass a complete annual hydrologic cycle starting when streamflow begins to increase from its annual minimum. The U.S. Geological Survey uses a water year that starts on October 1 and ends on September 30, and is designated by the year in which it ends.

Water-surface slope or gradient—The fall or head drop divided by the horizontal length of a reach or subreach.

Width-to-depth ratio—The width of streamflow or a channel cross section divided by the respective depth. In hydraulics, the top width and hydraulic depth are often used to compute the width-to-depth ratio.

Appendix A

CROSS-SECTION ROUGHNESS VALUES

Manning n values for all cross sections were determined using one of two general methods. The method used depended on how different the roughness characteristics were in comparison to a nearby cross section. Five cross sections were initially located in the Loop C study reach and in the combined Upper and Lower Loop D study reaches, and were numbered accordingly (01, 02, ..., 05). These original 10 cross sections were located where bed-material size or channel geometry was observed to change significantly. For these 10 cross sections, n values were estimated using the full suite of procedures described below (Method 1). Afterwards, it became necessary to locate additional cross sections within all three study reaches to facilitate either slope-area or standard step modeling. These additional cross sections (designated using labels like 1D, 3B, US, or DS) often exhibited roughness characteristics that were similar to all or a portion of a nearby, original cross section. In cases where roughness characteristics were similar, n values for the additional cross sections were extrapolated (Method 2) from those estimated for the nearby original cross section; in cases where they differed, n values were estimated for the additional cross sections using Method 1. Table A.1 lists how n values were derived for all of the cross sections used in this study.

Initial Manning n roughness values were estimated using the "Modified Channel Method" of Arcement and Schneider (1989) which computes a weighted mean n value for each subsection of a cross section. During survey field work and by visual inspection afterwards, a set of different cover types were identified that best matched the surface conditions existing before the 11 June event. These cover types represent the predominant ground cover affecting surface roughness (e.g., pavement, short grass, dense forest—see fig. 10). The cover types used are listed in table A.2. For the left- and right-overbank subsections, the following steps were taken to compute a single n value for each subsection.

1. Each subsection was subdivided into segments consisting of a single cover type.

2. The total slope length for each cover type along the subsection was computed.

3. Base n values were assigned to each cover type (table A.2).

4. Adjustments based on Arcement and Schneider (1989) were applied as needed to base n values for each cover type to account for surface irregularities, obstructions, and vegetation growth occurring along the ground surface and which varied by cross section. These adjustments are listed in table A.3 for cross sections in the Upper and Lower Loop D study reaches, and table A.4 for cross sections in the Loop C study reach. An adjusted n value was computed for each segment using equation A-1 (Arcement and Schneider 1989).

$$n = (n_b + n_1 + n_2 + n_3 + n_4) \qquad \text{(A-1)}$$

where

n_b = a base n value for the cover type
n_1 = adjustment for surface irregularities
n_2 = adjustment for cross section variation (assumed to equal 0 for all cross sections in this study)
n_3 = adjustment for obstructions
n_4 = adjustment for vegetation

5. A weighted mean n value (n_w) was computed for the entire subsection using the adjusted n values weighted by total segment length for each cover type segment (equation A-2).

$$n_w = \frac{\sum P_i n_i}{\sum P_i} \qquad \text{(A-2)}$$

where

P_i = total segment length for i-th cover type
n_i = adjusted n value for i-th cover type

For the main-channel subsections, the base n values were determined in a different manner. First, the bankfull elevation was used to divide the subsection into three segments: (1) the left-upper bank, (2) bankfull channel, and (3) right-upper bank. Using the channel distance and elevation of bankfull indicators determined during the field survey, simple linear regression was used to model the bankfull elevation throughout each study reach and to predict bankfull elevation at each cross section and subdivide the subsection into its three segments. The observed bankfull elevation models are shown in figure A.1 along with the predicted bankfull elevations for the 01-05 cross sections in all study reaches.

In all three study reaches, the left- and right-upper banks of the main channel had continuous forest cover, which varied in density and composition. Since the cover type was essentially the same, a single n value was selected for each upper-bank segment, but the value varied depending on stem density and size. The values used are listed in table A.5. No adjustments were made to these base n values for the upper-bank segments.

For the bankfull channel segment, the base n value was estimated using a representative value from a set of seven different predictions of the Manning n value. The predictive equations are taken from the literature and are based on theoretical or empirical models for estimating n values in coarse-bed channels based on various metrics for water-surface slope, channel geometry, and bed material size. The equations are listed in table A.6.

Bed-material metrics were determined from size distributions for the sampling segments in which the cross sections occurred. See figures 2 and 3 for segment locations, and figures 6 and 7 for size-distribution plots. The hydraulic radius and top width were calculated at the bankfull elevation for each cross section as the predictive equations were all developed for flows within the bankfull channel area. The energy slope used is that estimated for bankfull flow (i.e., the bankfull elevation change over channel distance). The base n values for all three segments in the main-channel subsections are listed in table A.5 along with their slope lengths and the variables used in the bankfull-channel prediction models. A weighted mean n value for the entire main-channel subsection was computed using equation (A-2), the base n values for the three segments, and their segment lengths.

The resulting initial estimates of n values for all subsections and cross sections are given in table 4. An example is given below to show how the estimates of n values are derived.

Example of Manning n Roughness Estimation for XS-D01

The XS-D01 cross section is divided into two subsections: the main channel and left overbank (fig. 5). The left-overbank subsection is covered by 5 different cover types; thus $i = 1$ to 5 in equation (A-2) where 1 = concrete or pavement; 2 = rocky forest soil; 3 = tall grass; 4 = short grass; and 5 = shrubs and small trees. The base Manning n values (n_b) for each cover type are taken from table A.2. For subsection segments with the concrete or pavement, or the shrubs and small trees cover types, no adjustments are needed for surface irregularities, obstructions, or

vegetation, thus $n_i = n_b$. The other three cover types are described in table A.7 along with their associated Manning n adjustments. Using equation (A-1), n_b values from table A.2, and the adjustments listed in table A.7, the adjusted n values are:

$$n_1 = 0.012$$
$$n_2 = (0.025 + 0.002 + 0.080) = 0.107$$
$$n_3 = (0.035 + 0.001 + 0.002) = 0.038$$
$$n_4 = (0.025 + 0.002) = 0.027$$
$$n_5 = 0.060$$

Using the adjusted n values above and the respective total segment lengths (in feet) for each cover type (table A.3), equation (A-2) is used to compute the weighted mean n value for the subsection:

$$n_w = \frac{0.012(42) = 0.107(128) + 0.038(41) + 0.027(35) + 0.060(66)}{42 + 128 + 41 + 35 + 66}$$

$$n_w = 0.066$$

This is the initial Manning n estimate listed for the left-overbank subsection of XS-D01 in table 4.

The main-channel subsection is divided into three segments: (1) the right-upper bank, (2) bankfull channel, and (3) left-upper bank. Both the right- and left-upper bank segments have fairly continuous shrub and forest cover, with vegetation density being somewhat greater on the right-upper bank. Manning n values for both segments are listed in table A.5.

Using the equations listed in table A.6 and the values for their respective variables listed in table A.5, the predictions of n for the bankfull-channel segment are:

$$n_{mpm} = 0.030$$
$$n_l = 0.044$$
$$n_s = 0.036$$
$$n_{jf} = 0.031$$
$$n_g = 0.036$$
$$n_j = 0.050$$
$$n_{bd} = 0.038$$

The median value of this data series ($n = 0.036$) was selected as the n estimate for the main-channel segment. This is the value listed in table A.5 for XS-D01.

Using equation (A-2) and the n values and respective lengths (in feet) for the three main-channel segments listed in table A.5, the weighted mean n value for the main-channel subsection is

$$n_w = 0.060(47) + 0.100(46) + 0.036(95)/(47 + 46 + 95)$$

$$n_w = 0.056$$

This is the initial Manning n estimate listed in table 4 for the main-channel subsection of XS-D01.

Table A.1—Method used for estimating subsection or segment Manning *n* values for cross sections in the Albert Pike Recreation Area study reaches

Study reach	Cross section	Left overbank	Left-upper bank	Bankfull channel	Right-upper bank	Right overbank
			Subsection			
			Main channel			
Upper Loop D	XS-DUS	Measured	Measured	XS-D01	Measured	—
	XS-D01	Measured	Measured	Measured	Measured	—
	XS-D1D	Measured	Measured	XS-D01	Measured	—
	XS-D1C	Measured	Measured	XS-D01	Measured	—
	XS-D02	Measured	Measured	Measured	Measured	—
	XS-D03	Measured	Measured	Measured	Measured	—
	XS-D3B	Measured	Measured	XS-D04	Measured	—
	XS-D3C	Measured	Measured	XS-D04	Measured	—
	XS-D04	Measured	Measured	Measured	Measured	—
Lower Loop D	XS-D05	Measured	Measured	Measured	Measured	—
	XS-DDS	Measured	Measured	XS-D05	Measured	—
Loop C	XS-CUS	XS-C01	XS-C01	XS-C01	XS-C01	—
	XS-C01	Measured	Measured	Measured	Measured	—
	XS-C1B	XS-C02	XS-C02	XS-C02	XS-C02	—
	XS-C02	Measured	Measured	Measured	Measured	—
	XS-C03	Measured	Measured	Measured	Measured	—
	XS-C3B	XS-C04	XS-C04	XS-C04	XS-C04	XS-C04
	XS-C04	Measured	Measured	Measured	Measured	Measured
	XS-C05	Measured	Measured	Measured	Measured	Measured

— = not applicable
"Measured" means the *n* value is based on measurements of individual cover type *n* values and slope lengths
"XS-xxx" indicates the cross section that was used to estimate the *n* value (e g XS-D01)

Table A.2—Base manning *n* values and adjustments for cover types used in modeling peak discharge for all cross sections in the Albert Pike Recreation Area study reaches

Cover type	Manning *n*	Base *n* source	Surface irregularity	Obstructions	Vegetation
Concrete or pavement	0.012	Arcement and Schneider (1989)	Not used	Not used	Not used
Rocky forest soil	0.025	Arcement and Schneider (1989)	0.000-0.005	0.000-0.009	0.005-0.080
Tall grass	0.035	Van Haveren (1986)	0.001	0.000	0.002-0.005
Short grass	0.025	Van Haveren (1986)	0.001-0.002	0.000-0.007	0.000-0.005
Shrubs and small trees	0.060	Van Haveren (1986)	Not used	Not used	Not used

Table A.3—Cover type slope lengths and adjustments used to estimate Manning n values for the left-overbank subsections in the Upper and Lower Loop D study reaches in the Albert Pike Recreation Area

Study reach	Cross section	Concrete or pavement		Rocky forest soil		Tall grass		Short grass		Shrubs and small trees	
		Slope length	Adjustment	Slope length	Adjustment	Slope length	Adjustment	Slope length	Adjustment	Slope length	Adjustment
		feet		feet		feet		feet		feet	
Upper Loop D	XS-DUS	23	0	225	0.082	40	0	0	0	0	0
	XS-D01	42	0	128	0.82	41	0.003	35	0.002	66	0
	XS-D1D	42	0	96	0.82	41	0.003	67	0	66	0
	XS-D1C	109	0	58	0.080	33	0.003	105	0	0	0
	XS-D02	123	0	57	0.080	45	0.003	86	0	0	0
	XS-D03	93	0	20	0.005	71	0.005	136	0	0	0
	XS-D3B	87	0	0	0	82	0.006	149	0	0	0
	XS-D3C	66	0	54	0.080	10	0.006	144	0.010	0	0
	XS-D04	58	0	27	0.080	0	0	182	0	0	0
Lower Loop D	XS-D05	78	0	89	0.010	0	0	51	0.006	0	0
	XS-DDS	37	0	93	0.010	0	0	86	0.006	0	0

Table A.4—Cover type slope lengths and adjustments used to estimate Manning n values for left- and right-overbank subsections in the Albert Pike Recreation Area Loop C study reach

Cross section	Left-overbank subsection				Right-overbank subsection			
	Concrete or pavement		Rocky forest soil		Concrete or pavement		Rocky forest soil	
	Slope length	Adjustment	Slope length	Adjustment	Slope length	Adjustment	Slope length	Adjustment
	feet		feet		feet		feet	
XS-C01	24	0	148	0.019	—	—	—	—
XS-C02	91	0	98	0.026	—	—	—	—
XS-C03	55	0	124	0.022	—	—	—	—
XS-C04	57	0	108	0.022	27	0	69	0.015
XS-C05	46	0	94	0.022	29	0	98	0.013

Table A.5—Base Manning *n* values for main-channel subsection segments in the Albert Pike Recreation Area study reaches, along with their slopes lengths and variables used to predict bankfull *n* values

Study reach	Cross section	Left-upper bank Slope length	Left-upper bank n	Right-upper bank Slope length	Right-upper bank n	D_{50}	D_{84}	D_{90}	Hydraulic radius	Bankfull channel Water-surface slope	Top width	n	Slope length
		feet		feet		------- mm -------			feet		feet		feet
Upper Loop D	XS-DUS	47	0.080	46	0.100	—	—	—	—	—	—	0.036[a]	95
	XS-D01	23	0.060	40	0.100	62	198	235	3.32	0.0045	92.95	0.036	96
	XS-D1D	23	0.100	40	0.100	—	—	—	—	—	—	0.036[a]	96
	XS-D1C	29	0.100	40	0.100	—	—	—	—	—	—	0.036[a]	89
	XS-D02	45	0.100	31	0.100	62	236	407	3.18	0.0045	71.95	0.036	85
	XS-D03	54	0.080	32	0.100	117	422	643	4.12	0.0045	71.59	0.042	74
	XS-D3B	49	0.080	27	0.100	—	—	—	—	—	—	0.038[b]	78
	XS-D3C	61	0.080	43	0.100	—	—	—	—	—	—	0.038[b]	79
	XS-D04	62	0.080	55	0.100	75	479	686	2.22	0.0045	99.77	0.038	101
Lower Loop D	XS-D05	73	0.100	19	0.100	113	375	614	4.08	0.0045	81.83	0.042	85
	XS-DDS	73	0.100	46	0.100	—	—	—	—	—	—	0.042[c]	78
Loop C	XS-C01	15	0.080	22	0.140	66	253	524	5.86	0.0042	101.72	0.037	107
	XS-C02	14	0.080	28	0.140	136	364	623	5.76	0.0042	112.08	0.046	120
	XS-C03	30	0.070	60	0.120	136	364	623	5.14	0.0042	98.42	0.046	106
	XS-C04	44	0.050	44	0.090	113	240	382	4.49	0.0042	86.48	0.041	91
	XS-C05	67	0.050	59	0.100	113	375	614	4.16	0.0042	85.81	0.041	83

— = not applicable.

[a] Uses the same bankfull channel base n value for XS-D01.

[b] Uses the same bankfull channel base n value for XS-D04.

[c] Uses the same bankfull channel base n value for XS-D05.

Table A.6—Equations used to predict Manning n values for bankfull channel areas in the Albert Pike Recreation Area study reaches

Source	Equation
Meyer-Peter and Muller (1948)[a]	$n_{mpm} = \dfrac{1}{26}(D_{90})^{\frac{1}{6}}$
Limerinos (1970)[b]	$n_l = \dfrac{0.0926 R^{\frac{1}{6}}}{1.16 + 2.00 \log \dfrac{R}{D_{84}}}$
Stickler (Shen and Julien 1993)[b]	$n_s = \dfrac{1}{21.1} D_{50}^{\frac{1}{6}}$
Jobson and Froehlich (1988)[b]	$n_{jf} = 0.245 R^{0.14} \dfrac{R^{-0.44}}{D_{50}} \dfrac{T^{-0.3}}{R}$
Griffiths (1981)[a]	$n_g = \dfrac{1.13 R^{\frac{1}{6}}}{0.76 + 1.98 \log \dfrac{R}{D_{50}}}$
Jarrett (1983)[b]	$n_j = 0.47 s^{0.38} R^{-0.16}$
Bray and Davar (1987)	$n_{bd} = 0.094 S^{\frac{1}{6}}$

n = Manning roughness va ue; R = hydrau ic radius; D_x = bed-materia diameter corresponding to the x percenti e of the size distribution; T = top width; S = energy s ope (dimension ess)

[a] Variab es measured in meters
[b] Variab es measured in feet

Table A.7—Manning n adjustments used for selected cover types at cross section XS-D01 in the Upper Loop D study reach in the Albert Pike Recreation area

Cover type	Description	Manning n adjustment		
		Surface irregularity	Obstructions	Vegetation
Tall grass	A few minor surface irregularities, no obstructions, and a few clumps of trees	0.001	0	0.002
Rocky forest soil	Moderately dense stand of mature, mixed pine-hardwoods, minor surface irregularities, and no obstructions	0.002	0	0.080
Short grass	Minor surface irregularities, no obstructions, and no shrubs or trees	0.002	0	0

Appendix B

EXCLUDED HIGH-WATER MARKS

Several high-water marks were excluded from the datasets used to model how high-water elevations changed with distance in the Loop C and combined Upper and Lower Loop D study reaches. For the right bank of the Loop C reach, the four marks that were excluded are shown in figure B.1 along with all other data. The four suspect marks all have elevations that are clearly different from the surrounding data points. For the two downstream-most marks, confidence in mark reliability is only rated as fair, whereas the one immediately downstream is rated excellent (a U.S. Geological Survey mark on a display case) and the next one upstream from the two is rated as good. The two suspect marks further upstream are similar in that they occur between marks with

good or excellent ratings, and do not seem to follow the trend apparent in other nearby marks. For these reasons, these four marks were excluded from the analysis.

For the right bank of the combined Loop D study reaches, two marks were excluded (fig. B.1). The mark near 630 feet downstream is a clear outlier. It was identified in an area where, in hindsight, flow conditions were probably disrupted by a significant change in valley geometry due to the construction of Forest Service Road 914 (fig. 3). This was a poor location for finding reliable high-water marks, even though at the time the mark was rated as fair. The other suspect mark at 240 feet downstream, though rated as good, does not match the clear trend apparent from all the surrounding upstream and downstream marks. Therefore these two marks were excluded.

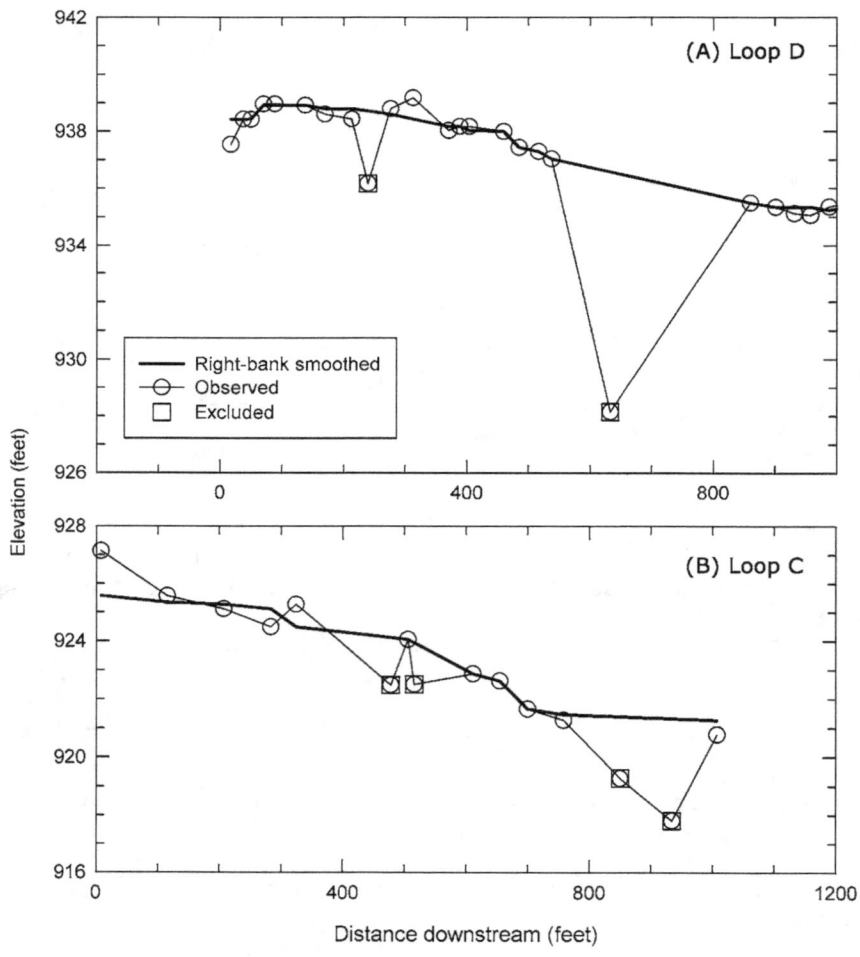

Figure B 1   High-water marks used and exc uded in mode ing right-bank high-water e evation change with distance for the June 11 2010 flood in the A bert Pike Recreation Area study reaches

Appendix C _____

SLOPE-AREA COMPUTATION REACHES

The recommend guidelines for identifying a suitable reach for applying the slope-area model (Benson and Dalrymple 1967; Dalrymple and Benson 1968) are listed below.

1. Good high-water marks are present

2. Channel geometry is as uniform and straight as possible within the modeled reach (trapezoidal shape, contracting in the downstream direction)

3. Channel geometry is uniform upstream of the modeled reach

4. Free overfalls do not occur

5. Meets one or more of the following conditions: (a) reach length ≥ 75 times mean flow depth; (b) fall in reach ≥ velocity head; or (c) fall in reach ≥ 0.5 foot

6. Significant scour or filling did not occur during the event

Guideline 6 was judged to be true throughout both the Loop C and Upper Loop D study reaches, so it did not play a role in locating the slope-area computation (SAC) reaches.

The location of the SAC reaches used in the Loop C and Upper Loop D study reaches was determined using the following process:

1. Three widely spaced, consecutive cross sections in each study reach were selected that appeared to meet guidelines 1-4, and the fall ≥ 0.5 feet condition of guideline 5.

2. The SAC program (Fulford 1994) was used to compute a model using the specific location, geometry, roughness, and HWE characteristics of the three cross sections. In addition to an overall peak discharge estimate, the SAC program computes a number of hydraulic diagnostic metrics that are used to judge how much confidence can be placed in the results of each slope-area computation.

3. The computed hydraulic metrics were evaluated based on guidelines given in Dalrymple and Benson (1984), Fulford (1994), and Kirby (1987). If this evaluation indicated a low degree of confidence in the model, the data for one of the cross sections was replaced with data from another cross section not previously used, and the three-step process was repeated. Alternatively, if the model diagnostics indicated serious problems for the entire candidate SAC reach, a completely different location was selected and three new

cross sections were used. This continued until an acceptable model was produced.

4. Once an acceptable model was produced, a new cross section was added to the dataset on either the upstream or downstream side, and the model was recomputed. This was done to produce the longest SAC reach possible. However, it was found that whenever more than three cross sections were used model quality was greatly degraded, thus the final SAC reaches utilize only three cross sections each.

The roughness values used for each cross section were the initial estimates of the Manning n values. Details on the derivation of the n-value estimates are given in appendix A, and the initial values used are listed in table 4.

A single high-water elevation (HWE) was used for each cross section included in the slope-area calculations. While the SAC program (Fulford 1994) can handle different left- and right-bank HWEs for each cross section, the differences in HWEs for individual cross sections were judged small enough that such modeling was not required. In situations where the reliability of high-water marks was similar between banks, an average of the left- and right-bank HWEs estimated for a given cross section was used as the single HWE. Where reliability differed, the HWE estimate from the bank side with the more reliable marks was used.

The SAC reach in the Loop C study reach is located between XS-C02, XS-C03, and XS-C04 (fig. 2). The HWEs used for slope-area model were taken from the right-bank for XS-C02 and XS-C04 because the right-bank data were judged more reliable for these two locations. For XS-C03, the difference between the estimated left- and right-bank HWEs was small (0.03 feet), so the average HWE was used. Diagnostics from the preliminary SAC model indicate that the SAC reach satisfied all but one of the guidelines listed above (table C.1). Good high-water marks were present, the fall between cross sections exceeded 0.5 foot, channel geometry was fairly uniform both within and upstream of the reach, and cross sections exhibited a trapezoidal shape through the reach (fig. 4). While top width increases from XS-C02 to XS-C04, cross-sectional area actually decreases in the downstream direction, indicating contraction through the SAC reach. Cross-section velocity heads were all somewhat higher than fall values, but not greatly so. Only the reach length guideline was severely violated, but this was true of all tested locations and could not be avoided.

The SAC reach in the Upper Loop D study reach is located between XS-D1C, XS-D02, and XS-D03 (fig. 3). Here, the average of the estimated left- and right-bank HWEs was

Table C.1—Diagnostic values used to identify slope-area computation reaches and preliminary discharge models. See Fulford (1994) for details on computation of diagnostic values

Study reach	Sub-reach	Fall	Length	Discharge	Spread	CX	RC	RX	Length: Depth > 75	Conveyance ratio	Maximum velocity head:fall	Friction head:fall
		--- feet ---		cfs	percent							
Loop C	C02-C03	1.34	165	47,600	0	1	0.111	0	No	1.21	1.25	0.90
	C03-C04	1.42	217	38,300	0	1	0.259	0	No	0.91	1.42	0.79
	All	2.76	382	42,100	0	1	0.199	0	No	1.10	0.73	0.83
Upper Loop D	D1C-D02	0.5	128	35,000	6	0.966	0.000	-0.124	No	0.99	2.46	1.07
	D02-D03	0.59	156	36,400	0	1	0.028	0	No	0.82	2.00	0.97
	All	1.09	284	35,700	3	0.984	0.014	-0.062	No	0.82	1.13	1.02

used at all three cross sections as the high-water marks on both sides seemed equally reliable. Model diagnostics indicate the Upper Loop D SAC reach is not as good as that in the Loop C study reach, but is still satisfactory (table C.1). The Upper Loop D SAC reach also exhibited good high-water marks, sufficient falls between cross sections, fairly uniform channel geometry within and upstream of the reach, and cross sections with trapezoidal shapes (fig. 5). Cross section velocity heads exceed fall values by even larger amounts than for the Loop C SAC reach, but this difference still does not seem unacceptable. Once again, the reach length guideline cannot be met in the SAC reach, nor could it elsewhere in the Upper Loop D study reach. However, the most serious concern is the expansion that occurs in the downstream direction. Nonetheless, the spread values and other measures of the expansion effect are still relatively low for the preliminary model, and the reach was judged suitable for slope-area modeling.

Appendix D _____

SLOPE-AREA MODEL SELECTION PROCESS

The initial slope-area analysis for the Loop C and Upper Loop D SAC reaches produced a model for each reach. Based on the Manning n values for these initial models, additional models were computed using the SAC program (Fulford 1994) and varying the n values of the left-overbank and main-channel subsections by increments of 0.002 units through a range of ±0.008 units. The ±0.008 range was chosen because it is approximately ±10 percent of the largest n values initially estimated for any of the subsections (table 4), which seemed a reasonable error range for investigating candidate models. The permutations of these n value changes produced 81 additional models for each reach. A set of criteria were then used to identify a subset of slope-area models for consideration in the best-model selection process. Candidate models were selected that met the criteria listed below.

Criteria for All Models
- Equivalent or better diagnostic values than the initial model (the one listed in table D-1 with no changes to the n values). Preferred diagnostic values (Dalrymple and Benson 1984, Fulford 1994, Kirby 1987) are listed below.[1]

  o Fall > 0.5 feet
  o Conveyance ratio between 0.80 and 1.25
  o Reach length > 75 times mean streamflow depth
  o Spread as near to 0 as possible (spread < 5 percent is considered "good," 5-10 percent is "fair," and > 25 percent is "poor")
  o CX as near to 1.0 as possible
  o RC as near to 0 as possible
  o RX as near to 0 as possible
  o Friction head-to-fall ratio < 1.0
  o Velocity head-to-fall ratio < 1.0
  o Froude number < 1.0

- Ratios of discharge difference (i.e., the difference between the calculated upstream and downstream subreach discharges) to overall (i.e., entire SAC reach) discharge that are smaller than the initial model.

Criteria for Loop C SAC Reach Models Only
- Overall discharges that are similar to the one computed by Holmes and Wagner (2011) of 40,100 cubic feet per second.
- Increased roughness in the main channel subsections along with reasonable changes in the left bank subsections. Preliminary Hydrologic Engineering Center River Analysis System (HEC-RAS) runs with a model discharge of 40,100 cubic feet per second indicated that increased roughness would produce HWEs that better match observed HWEs.

Criteria for Upper Loop D SAC Reach Models Only
- Overall discharge that is > 34,000 and < 37,000 cubic feet per second. This is based on the reasoning that if peak discharge at the Loop C study reach is approximately 40,500 cubic feet per second and Brier Creek peak discharge is approximately 6,530 cubic feet per second (Holmes and Wagner 2011), then the maximum discharge in the Little Missouri River (LMR) upstream of Brier Creek would be approximately 34,000 cubic feet per second if the Brier Creek peak was coincidental with the LMR peak, or around 37,000 cubic feet per second if the Brier Creek was not at peak discharge, but instead was flowing at 3,500 cubic feet per second (about half of its estimated peak discharge).

Based on these criteria, the models listed in table D-1 were selected. The subsection n value changes and computed discharge for each model were then used in a standard step analysis to assess how well the computed HWEs matched the estimated HWEs at each cross section in the Loop C and Upper Loop D study reaches.

_____

[1]Preferred values for spread, CX, RX, and RC diagnostics were obtained through personal communication. Holmes, R.R. 2010. National Flood Specialist, U.S. Geological Survey, 1400 Independence Road, Rolla, MO 65401.

Table D.1—Overall and subreach discharge predictions from candidate models identified for the slope-area computation reaches in the Loop C and Upper Loop D study reaches of the Albert Pike Recreation Area. Models are identified by the change in Manning _n_ value applied to each subsection in the reach. The models listed as "+0.000" and "+0.000" under the Left overbank and Main channel headings, respectively, are the initial models identified for the slope-area computation reaches. Values for the selected models are highlighted

SAC[a] reach	Manning _n_ change		Discharge				Subreach difference as percent of overall discharge
	Left-overbank	Main channel	Overall	Upstream subreach	Downstream subreach	Subreach difference	
			cubic feet per second				percent
Loop C	+0.000	+0.000	42,100	47,600	38,300	9,300	22.1
	+0.002	+0.004	40,200	45,300	36,800	8,500	21.1
	+0.000	+0.004	40,800	45,400	37,500	7,900	19.4
	-0.002	+0.004	41,400	45,500	38,400	7,100	17.1
Upper Loop D	+0.000	+0.000	35,700	35,000	36,400	1,400	3.9
	-0.002	+0.002	34,600	34,800	34,500	300	0.9
	-0.002	+0.000	35,600	35,600	35,700	100	0.3

[a] SAC=slope area computation

www.ingramcontent.com/pod-product-compliance
Lightning Source LLC
Chambersburg PA
CBHW081114280526

45787CB00007B/2825